LIES MY PASTOR TOLD ME

Cole Brown

Copyright © 2010 Cole Brown / Humble Beast Records
3rd Edition copyright © 2018
All rights reserved.
ISBN 10: 1724719602
ISBN 13: 978-1724719607

All rights reserved. No part of this publication may be reproduced, distributed, or transmitted in any form or by any means, including photocopying, recording, or other electronic or mechanical methods, without the prior written permission of the publisher, except in the case of brief quotations embodied in critical reviews and certain other noncommercial uses permitted by copyright law. For permission requests, write to the publisher, addressed "Attention: Permissions Coordinator", at the email below.

Special discounts are available on quantity purchases by corporations, associations, ministries and others. For details, contact the publisher at hola@colebrown.es.

Scriptures taken from the Holy Bible, New International Version®, NIV®. Copyright © 1973, 1978, 1984, 2011 by Biblica, Inc.™ Used by permission of Zondervan. All rights reserved worldwide. www.zondervan.com The "NIV" and "New International Version" are trademarks registered in the United States Patent and Trademark Office by Biblica, Inc.™

To my wife, for living through this experience with me and never settling for less than God's truth.

TABLE OF CONTENTS

A Note to Leaders	i

INTRODUCTION TO THIRD EDITION	1
INTRODUCTION TO FIRST EDITION Discussion Guide 9	5
DON'T PUT YOUR MOUTH ON THE MAN OF GOD Discussion Guide 17	11
THE BIBLE IS GOD'S RULEBOOK Discussion Guide 23	19
THIS IS GOD'S HOUSE Discussion Guide 31	25
I FEEL THE SPIRIT Discussion Guide 37	33
I HAVE PEACE ABOUT THIS DECISION Discussion Guide 43	39
GOD WANTS YOU TO BE RICH Discussion Guide 49	45
THAT WILL MAKE YOU SIN Discussion Guide 55	51
SPEAK IT INTO EXISTENCE Discussion Guide 61	57

**YOU'RE NOT FILLED WITH THE SPIRIT
IF YOU DON'T SPEAK IN TONGUES**   63
Discussion Guide 71

THAT'S THE DEVIL   73
Discussion Guide 79

GOD HEALS ALL WHO HAVE FAITH   81
Discussion Guide 87

YOU HAVE A GENERATIONAL CURSE   89
Discussion Guide 95

SHE'S NOT ANOINTED   97
Discussion Guide 101

JUST BELIEVE GOD   103
Discussion Guide 107

DOCTRINE IS DANGEROUS   109
Discussion Guide 113

YOU DON'T HAVE TO BE PART OF A CHURCH   115
Discussion Guide 123

SIN IS SIN   125
Discussion Guide 131

**GOD WON'T PUT MORE ON YOU THAN
YOU CAN BEAR**   133
Discussion Guide 137

Frequently Asked Questions

A NOTE TO LEADERS

We are honored you have chosen to lead a group study of <u>Lies My Pastor Told Me: Confronting 18 Church Cliché's with the Gospel</u>. We have seen fruit from reading and discussing this book in our own lives and designed this material to help other small groups experience the same. We hope this new discussion guide will help facilitate thoughtful engagement with God's Word for you and your community. Before you begin, we hope you'll consider a few tips on how to make the most of your group study.

1. <u>Lay the Ground Rules</u>
   Make sure the group knows up front that the Scriptures will be treated as the ultimate authority in all discussions. Cole's book may be interesting, but his claims must be evaluated by the authority of Scripture. Group members' insights and convictions may be deeply held, but their claims must be evaluated by the authority of Scripture. Make sure people know up front that you are not asking them to submit to Cole's views nor to your own views. You are asking everyone to submit to the Scriptures. As such, it's wise to keep your Bibles open as you talk through the ideas in this book.

2. <u>Plan for Disagreement</u>
   While all may agree that Scripture is the ultimate authority it is likely that all won't agree on exactly how Scripture should be interpreted

and applied. Warn your group up-front, and repeatedly, that disagreement is to be expected. Agree beforehand on how you will handle such disagreements. Perhaps begin each session with a reading and meditation on Colossians 3:12-14 to encourage patience, humility and love.

3. <u>Pray for Unity and Revelation</u>
   Contrary to what many claim, doctrine is not divisive. Only false doctrine is divisive (1 Timothy 6:3-4). Thus, one goal of these discussions is to find unity through the truths of God's Word. Of course, such truths are never discovered through study alone. We human beings are simply too proud and foolish to be awakened by mere study, not to mention the evil forces that resist our enlightenment (2 Timothy 2:25-26). We need God's supernatural revelation to awaken us. As such, pray for your group regularly and pray specifically for God to bring unity to your group and revelatory power to reject lies and embrace truth.

Enjoy the study and let us know how it goes,

CJ Quartlbaum (@CJ_Quartlbaum)
Cole Brown (@colebrownpdx)

INTRODUCTION TO THIRD EDITION

Having your deeply held beliefs challenged is not fun.

Having your religious convictions and affections reshaped is not comfortable.

I know this, because I spent several years living through it.

Before writing this book, I lived this book. The teachings I call "lies" in this book are teachings I personally believed. These teachings helped determine how I saw God, myself, others, and how I lived my life. The arguments I use in this book to correct these teachings are arguments I personally heard from Scripture and from other Christians, which forced me to question and eventually abandon what I believed. The entire process was a painfully traumatic one for me.

This is why, in 2010, I began writing a series of blog posts examining popular church clichés in light of the Bible. The initial motivation, I confess, was entirely selfish. I simply needed to process on paper the trauma I had gone through in reality. That was my only intent until Thomas Terry, founder of Humble Beast Records, convinced me these posts could serve a broader purpose than my own catharsis. He believed they could encourage those in the middle of the same process and help free those who, like me, were unknowingly holding to harmful beliefs they assumed to be biblical. With this goal, Humble Beast released <u>Lies My Pastor Told Me: Confronting 15 Church Clichés with the Gospel</u> as an eBook in July of 2010.

It turned out that Thomas was right.

For the next few years we regularly heard reports from people all over the world who read the book. Many were comforted to find they were not alone in their journey through false teaching, others were awakened to the gospel's superiority over the false teaching they'd been believing, and still others were challenged to join gospel-centered churches where they could grow in the truth. This is one reason we're excited to release a third edition, in hopes that more can experience the same.

Of course, that's not to say that all the responses were positive. There were also many offended by the book and even reports of pastors preaching entire sermons against the book and against me, at least twice going so far as to accuse me of leading people to Hell. Far more helpful were the responses of those who appreciated much of the truth found in the book, but wished the truth would have been communicated differently. This is a second reason we're excited to release a new edition, in hopes of communicating the truths of the book with some of that feedback in mind.

To that end, this edition includes several changes from the originally released book.

1. We have added three chapters: "You Don't Have to Be Part of a Church," "Sin is Sin," and "God Won't Put More On You Than You Can Bear."

These chapters provide additional insight into how damaging false teaching is, how freeing the gospel is, and how necessary local church membership is - even after you've been deceived or hurt by one.

2. We have edited the language and content of each of the original chapters. In doing so, we tried to remove unnecessarily sharp language where possible, simplify arguments where possible, and provide further clarification on why these teachings matter where necessary.

3. We have added a Frequently Asked Questions section to the end of the book. We have found there are four questions readers often ask after finishing the book, and we address those questions in the FAQ section. It may actually be helpful for you to start there, as it will provide some helpful context for what you read in the following pages.

1. We have added a discussion guide for use in small groups. Our belief is that small groups are the ideal context for reading and discussing this book. They provide the necessary support for those who are going through the trauma of re-evaluating their beliefs. They also provide the influence of Christian community which helps guard against the personal pride and self-righteousness that can come when one discovers they have "right doctrine" and others do not. Most importantly, small groups help you evaluate the teaching of the Church as a part of the Church, rather than as one outside of it or above it.

We know you may be reading this book for any number of reasons and from the background of your own unique experiences. Whatever the reason and whatever your background, our biggest prayer is that in its pages you will see the beauty of the gospel of Jesus Christ and be moved to worship him. This is the ultimate purpose of doing theology.

INTRODUCTION TO FIRST EDITION

You may find the title of this book offensive. Perhaps you are wondering why I would choose to write an entire book on this topic and why I would use such strong language in doing so. The following illustration might help put things in perspective.

Imagine you are feeling ill. You have a number of symptoms but you do not have the formal training or medical knowledge to confidently diagnose yourself. So you go to the one person who does: your doctor. You tell your doctor you are experiencing pain in your chest, shortness of breath, dizziness and a cold sweat. These are the symptoms of a heart attack but your doctor does not bother to mention that, or offer any sort of treatment. Instead, he simply says, "An apple a day will keep the doctor away" and dismisses you. At the potential cost of your life the doctor has offered you nothing more than a cliché, a false cliché at that.

What would be your response? I imagine you would be angry and even demand he no longer be allowed to practice medicine. Such a response would be justified, considering you have entrusted your physical health to this doctor precisely because he claims to be qualified for the job. Should you be any less angry when you hear a false cliché from the mouth of the pastor to whom you have entrusted your spiritual health for the same reason?

Of course not.

You should be even angrier because believing a lie about God is all the more damaging than believing a lie about your physical health. It impacts your relationship with God, your relationship with others, your emotions, your behavior – everything. I know this from personal experience. I spent most of my twenties believing such lies and, while I did not realize it at the time, I lived in fear, pride and bondage as a result. To put it plainly, all lies are damaging but the most damaging lie of all is a lie about God. If you don't believe me just ask Adam and Eve.

This is why a book like this is both warranted and necessary, even if the title may offend some. It is not that I have an interest in attacking any particular pastor. In fact, the pastor I refer to throughout this book is not a specific individual but a composite character based on many pastors I have known over the past twelve years. In many cases these pastors are not intentionally lying but simply saying what they believe to be true by repeating the clichés they have heard throughout their lives. Nevertheless, they must be held to account because, intentional or not, they are doing significant damage to those who have entrusted their souls to them.

In short, this book is not written *against* those pastors who lie, it is written *for* those people who are lied to, that they might get a fresh glimpse of who God is and experience the joy and freedom that results. To this end I have divided the book into 15 chapters, each focusing on a common church cliché. Every chapter consists of three basic parts:

    1)   A brief explanation of the cliché.

2) An examination of what Scripture truly teaches on the subject.

3) An explanation of how the teachings of Scripture clearly give Jesus more glory and do you more good than the church cliché that is so often quoted.

Since every chapter was written to stand on its own it is not necessary to read the book in sequence. But I do recommend you read chapter 1 first as it provides the foundation for all that follows.

Let's begin by confronting one of the most dangerous lies of all...

DISCUSSION GUIDE: INTRODUCTION

CHAPTER SUMMARY
This book is not written *against* pastors who lie, but *for* those who have been lied to. The goal of the book is to give believers a fresh glimpse of who God is and to experience the joy and freedom that results.

DISCUSSION QUESTIONS

1. What emotional reaction do you have to the title of this book? Why?

2. Based on what you know about the book already, what fears or concerns do you have about the upcoming study?

3. If you are currently believing something false about God and his truth do you want to know that you are wrong? Why or why not?

4. What would be some potential benefits of finding out you believe something false about God? What would be some potential risks of discovering that?

DON'T PUT YOUR MOUTH ON THE MAN OF GOD

I can't begin a book titled Lies My Pastor Told Me without first addressing the claim that Christian preachers should never be critiqued. Many Christian leaders (and their followers) assert that it is both dangerous and sinful to say anything negative about a Christian minister or his teaching. As my pastor would repeatedly warn, "Don't put your mouth on the man of God!"

It is both biblical and wise to exercise caution before critiquing a pastor's life or teaching (1 Timothy 5:19). Yet pastors (including myself) are not beyond being critiqued. We know this, firstly, because the scripture most often used to defend this claim does not actually mean what many say it means. Those who warn you to not "put your mouth on the man of God" frequently defend their position by pointing to Psalm 105:15, "Do not touch my anointed ones; do my prophets no harm." Those who appeal to this verse see it as a direct command to neither touch nor harm "God's man" in any way – including criticism. To reach this interpretation, though, they have to ignore the immediate context of Psalm 105 and the extended context of the entire Bible.

When we read Psalm 105 in its entirety it is evident that the "anointed ones" are not pastors. Nor are the "anointed ones" kings or prophets. The author of Psalm 105 uses the phrase "anointed ones" to refer to the people of God as a whole. In the New Testament every Christian is one of the "anointed ones." In the context of Psalm 105, though, the "anointed ones" are the people of Israel. This is clear even if we start reading just a few verses earlier,

> "When they were but few in number,
> few indeed, and strangers in it,
> they wandered from nation to nation,
> from one kingdom to another.
> He allowed no one to oppress them;
> for their sake he rebuked kings:
> 'Do not touch my anointed ones;
> do my prophets no harm.'"
> (Psalm 105:12-15)

The author of Psalm 105 is not attempting to tell us that we should not criticize leaders or ministers. In fact, the author of Psalm 105 is not primarily telling us anything about *us* at all. Instead, the author of Psalm 105 is primarily telling us about God and his great faithfulness to his people. His defense of his people, Israel, is one example of that.

Just as Psalm 105 does not prohibit us from appropriately critiquing Christian leaders, neither does the rest of Scripture. In fact, the Bible gives us numerous examples of godly people critiquing both the life and doctrine of prominent leaders. For instance, in 1 Samuel 24:8-15 we read of a public confrontation between David and King Saul, his superior at the time. David yells out to Saul and confesses that it would not be right of him to physically harm Saul, because he is God's king. But David does not believe that it would be unjust of him to expose Saul's sin. So he openly rebukes Saul for his evil heart and actions and calls for God to avenge the wrongs Saul has done to David.

In Galatians 2:11-14 we encounter another example of a godly man publicly critiquing his superior. In this case it is the Apostle Paul rebuking the Apostle Peter for not living in line with the truth of the gospel. Paul did not do this privately. He did it publicly. According to the text he did this "in front of them all" because the truth of the gospel had to be protected. It was not a sin for Paul to expose Peter's error publicly. It would have been a sin for Paul to allow Peter and others to walk out of step with the gospel without exposing their error publicly.

We could point to many more examples of godly people critiquing the life and doctrine of leaders and ministers (such as Nathan rebuking David for his immorality, Jesus repeatedly exposing the religious leaders as blind guides, Paul identifying Hymenaeus and Alexander as false teachers etc...) but we do not need to. Even without these examples we can be assured that the Bible does not forbid critiquing the life and doctrine of Christian leaders because, far from commanding us not to do such a thing, the Bible actually commands us to do that very thing. Below are just a few of the many passages that tell us to correct false teachers and their false teachings:

> "(An elder) must hold firmly to the trustworthy message as it has been taught, so that he can encourage others by sound doctrine and refute those who oppose it" (Titus 1:9).

> "For there are many rebellious people, full of meaningless talk and deception...They must be silenced, because they are disrupting whole

households by teaching things they ought not to teach..." (Titus 1:10-11).

"But avoid foolish controversies and genealogies and arguments and quarrels about the law, because these are unprofitable and useless. Warn divisive people once, and then warn them a second time. After that, have nothing to do with them. You may be sure that such people are warped and sinful; they are self-condemned" (Titus 3:9-11).

"I felt compelled to write you and urge you to contend for the faith that the Lord has once for all entrusted to us, his people. For certain individuals whose condemnation was written about long ago have secretly slipped in among you. They are ungodly people, who pervert the grace of our God into a license for immorality and deny Jesus Christ our only Sovereign and Lord" (Jude 3b-4).

"Have nothing to do with the fruitless deeds of darkness, but rather expose them" (Ephesians 5:11).

My pastor said, "Don't put your mouth on the man of God" because he wanted me to believe he was above critique. The clear message of the Bible, however, is that none of us is above critique because none of us is the ultimate authority – God is. Anytime our life or doctrine contradicts God's Word we open ourselves up to correction. If we value God's Word then we will gladly receive that correction and submit ourselves to the Scriptures. In the same way, if we value God's Word, we will correct others when their life or doctrine is not in line with God's revelation in the Scriptures. We do not do this to humiliate people but to help people and the people they influence by pointing them to Jesus and his gospel.

That is what I am attempting to do in this book.

DISCUSSION GUIDE: DON'T PUT YOUR MOUTH ON THE MAN OF GOD

CHAPTER SUMMARY
Incorrect use of Psalm 105 has led many to believe that church leaders are always beyond questioning. Scripture contradicts this claim by repeatedly showing us that certain deviations from God's will must be confronted.

DISCUSSION QUESTIONS
1. Why do you think so many pastors (and laypeople) use Psalm 105:15 incorrectly?

2. Is it ever appropriate to confront a pastor or elder concerning their sin? Why or why not? If appropriate, what would be the proper way to approach a pastor or elder concerning their sin?

3. What are some examples of areas in which we can confront a pastor or elder?

4. How do you balance the biblical command to rebuke false teachers with the biblical command to submit to your leaders?

THE BIBLE IS GOD'S RULEBOOK

My pastor taught me to read the Bible as a book of rules. "This is God's rulebook!" he would repeatedly say. Now, because the Bible is in fact filled with hundreds of direct commands my pastor's statement has the appearance of being true. But it isn't true. Though the Bible has much to say about how we are to live, it is not primarily about how we are to live. To sum up the Bible as God's rulebook, or as God's playbook, or the owner's manual to life is to sum up the Bible wrongly.

Yet this view of the Bible remains a common one. It's not only seen in the language we use to describe the Bible, but also in how we teach the Bible. Even many who would never call the Bible "God's rulebook" still treat it as not much more than that. In many churches the sermons preached are primarily about what you're doing wrong, what you should be doing right, and how to do it. The clear emphasis of such sermons is on you and what you must do in order to receive God's blessing. This gives the impression that the Bible exists for the primary purpose of telling us how to live a moral life in order that we might also live the good life. In other words, seeing the Bible as God's Rulebook also causes us to see the Bible as a book that is first and foremost about us.

But it is not.

The Bible is not first and foremost about us. To the contrary, the Bible is first and foremost about God. It is his self-revelation in written form and its primary purpose is to tell us about his self-revelation in the physical form of Jesus Christ. But don't take my word for it. Listen to Jesus, who rebuked his disciples for not recognizing that all of the Scriptures revealed him and, "…beginning with Moses and all the Prophets, he explained to them what was said in all the Scriptures concerning himself" (Luke 24:27).

Listen to Jesus who rebuked the religious leaders for seeing the Scriptures as a book primarily about how they should live instead of as a book about who Jesus is: "You diligently study the Scriptures because you think that by them you possess eternal life. These are the Scriptures that testify about me, yet you refuse to come to me to have life" (John 5:39).

Listen to Jesus who claims that the Old Testament scriptures are not fulfilled by who we are or what we do but by who he is and what he has done: "Do not think that I have come to abolish the Law or the Prophets; I have not come to abolish them but to fulfill them" (Matthew 5:17).

Clearly, Jesus does not see the Bible as a mere book of rules. Jesus sees the Bible as God's written form of self-revelation whose primary purpose is to testify to God's ultimate self-revelation in the person and work of Jesus Christ.

This does not, however, mean the rules or commands of the Bible are unimportant. They are exceedingly important because they, like the rest of the Bible, serve the Bible's primary purpose of revealing God. They do this in at least three ways.

First, the rules and commands of the Bible reveal God to us by showing us his character as the lawgiver. As we look at his laws we learn the lawgiver is holy, pure, faithful, just, righteous, and patient. In other words, God does not call us to be holy simply because he has the power to do so. He calls us to be holy because he himself is holy. As he explains to Moses and the Israelites, "I am the Lord your God; consecrate yourselves and be holy, because I am holy" (Leviticus 11:44). Unlike the rules found in many employee manuals, the rules found in God's Word are not arbitrary. Instead, God's commands flow naturally from who he is and what he values.

Second, the rules and commands of the Bible reveal God to us by showing us where we stand in relation to him. According to the Scriptures, the Biblical law was not given to us so we could know how to get right with God. Rather, the law was given to us so we could see that we are utterly incapable of getting right with God. As Paul writes, "...through the law we become conscious of our sin" (Romans 3:20b) and, as we are made aware of our sin, we are also made aware that this failure to obey the law "brings wrath" (Romans 4:15). In short, the law reveals God to be our enemy whose condemnation we deserve.

Third, the rules and commands of the Bible reveal God to us by pointing us to Jesus Christ. After the law leads us to recognize God's character and our enmity with him, it also leads us to recognize our desperate need for someone who *has* kept God's law to mediate between us and him. And this is no coincidence. This is the purpose for which God designed the law to begin with. Paul explains, "...the law was put in charge of us until Christ came that we might be justified by faith. Now that this faith has come, we are no longer under the supervision of the law" (Galatians 3:24-25). From the very beginning, God intended that the law would expose our sin, make us aware of our impending judgment, and point us to Jesus Christ – the fulfillment of the law – for rescue and rest.

There is no question the Bible is filled with rules and commands. But the Bible is not *about* these rules and commands. The Bible is about the Triune God, and even its rules and commands are designed to reveal him to us and drive us to him in faith and worship. We must, therefore, reject "biblical teaching" that is only about what we are supposed to do, how we are supposed to do it, and how it will benefit us if we do. These sermons are not Christian sermons. They are sermons that could just as easily be preached in a Mormon Temple, a Muslim Mosque, or on your daytime talkshow of choice. Christian sermons are those that proclaim Jesus' person and work as the fulfillment of every command, the reason to obey every command, and the means by which you can obey every command. Such sermons rightly handle the Bible not as God's Rulebook but as God's self-revelation to human beings.

DISCUSSION GUIDE: THE BIBLE IS GOD'S RULEBOOK

CHAPTER SUMMARY
The Bible is not God's rulebook. It is His revelation of himself to us. The focus of the Bible is not on our morality but on the person and work of Jesus Christ and on knowing and loving him.

DISCUSSION QUESTIONS
1. Have you ever heard the Bible described using any of the metaphors mentioned in this chapter (such as a rulebook, a gameplan for life, an owner's manual etc...)?

2. What is the biggest danger of viewing the Bible in the ways above?

3. How does this affect the way a Pastor preaches?

4. If we approach the Bible expecting to find Jesus on every page how might that change the way we read it and use it?

5. How do we find Jesus in those passages that do not explicitly mention Jesus (i.e. much of the Old Testament)?

THIS IS GOD'S HOUSE

My pastor used to esteem the building we met in for Sunday service as "God's house." Because this facility was considered to be God's house we had to dress, speak, and act differently than we would in any other public place. I always wondered why my house was nicer than God's house and why he couldn't even get a house with clean and working bathrooms. I've come to learn that this is because neither our church building nor any other church building is actually God's holy and unique dwelling place.

In the Old Testament the people of Israel worshiped God at the temple in Jerusalem. The temple *was* a holy and unique place. God *did* refer to it as "my house" (1 Chronicles 28:6). It was specifically here that God dwelt with his people and made his presence known to them and it was specifically here that the people came to worship God with their sacrifices and offerings (2 Chronicles 6). As such, the temple was central to the Jewish religion.

Jesus, of course, was a faithful Jew. It should not, therefore, surprise us to find that Jesus spoke of the temple with great respect. He called it, "My Father's house" (John 2:16), and because it was God's house Jesus considered everything in it to be holy (Matthew 23:19-22). For this reason he was indignant when he saw the temple being used as a place of profit, so much so that he drove out the moneychangers with a whip while proclaiming, "It is written, 'My house will be a house of prayer'; but you have made it a 'den of robbers'" (Luke 19:46).

Jesus was unquestionably zealous for God's house, the temple. This is precisely what makes his other statements about the temple so shocking. Speaking of himself, Jesus said, "I tell you that one greater than the temple is here" (Matthew 12:6). On the one hand Jesus exalted the temple as the holy dwelling place of God. On the other hand Jesus claimed that he was superior to the temple. How could this be? How could both be true? The answer is found in John 2:18-22. After he drove the religious profiteers from the temple the people asked, "What sign can you show us to prove your authority to do all this?" Jesus' response was prophetic: "Destroy this temple, and I will raise it again in three days." His Jewish audience thought he was crazy and they mocked him accordingly. "It has taken forty-six years to build this temple, and you are going to raise it in three days?" What they failed to understand was that Jesus was not speaking about the temple as they knew it: a building built with hands. He was speaking of his own body. And he wasn't crazy. Three days after the Jews destroyed Jesus' body the same Jesus rose from the dead in a glorified version of the same body.

This is why Jesus was able simultaneously to esteem the temple and claim to be greater than the temple. Because Jesus *was* and *is* the temple. Jesus, of course, is not the temple made of stones; he is the fulfillment of the temple made of stones. Jesus is the True and Perfect Temple. The stone temple, in all of its glory, was a mere shadow of the far greater reality found only in Jesus (Colossians 2:17). While God temporarily dwelt in the temple made of stone, God eternally dwells in Jesus, the True and Perfect Temple. While God was once accessible only to those who could come to the stone temple in Jerusalem,

God is now accessible to any and all who come to Jesus, the True and Perfect Temple. While people once worshiped God at a specific location people now worship God at any location by coming to Jesus, the True and Perfect Temple.

Because Jesus is the True and Perfect Temple, those who are in Christ — those who are united to him through faith — have together also become a temple. This is astounding: because of Christ, we sinners have together become the dwelling place of God! Peter says this about the Church (meaning the gathered people of God and not a building), "As you come to him, the living Stone — rejected by human beings but chosen by God and precious to him — you also, like living stones, are being built into a spiritual house…" (1 Peter 2:4-5). Also speaking of the Church, Paul explains, "Don't you know that you yourselves are God's temple and that God's Spirit dwells in your midst? If anyone destroys God's temple, God will destroy that person; for God's temple is sacred, and you together are that temple" (1 Corinthians 3:16-17). Because Jesus is the True and Perfect Temple the gathered Church has also become a temple where God dwells through his Holy Spirit and where God is worshiped and made known to the world.

Thus, it is inappropriate to refer to any building as "God's house." While it is true that all things belong to God it is not true that God reserves his presence for particular buildings with particular architectural qualities and a minimum number of pews. *Jesus is God's house.* And because of our unity with Jesus, the Christian Church is God's house (again, when we speak of "the Church" we are not speaking of a building, we are speaking about the people who worship Jesus gathered together - which is often inside of a building).

This all may seem like a fairly minor theological point. And in the grand scheme of things it may be. But it's not unimportant. In fact, it is essential that we distinguish between what modern Christians often call "God's house" and what the New Testament calls "God's house." Why? Because whatever you call "God's house" will determine where you go to find God.

If we want to draw near to God, we need to know that he is found in Jesus and in his gathered church. If we want to behold God's majesty, we need to know that his majesty is found in Jesus and in his gathered church. If we want other people to see God for who he is, we must bring them to Jesus and to his gathered church. This does not mean that God is not present elsewhere, it just means he is not present elsewhere in the same special way.

This tells us that Jesus and his gathered church are essential for knowing God and showing God, but a certain type of building is not. We are now able to worship God and experience his presence anywhere and everywhere simply by turning to Jesus in faith and gathering with his people in worship. This is precisely the way Jesus promised it would be when he taught the woman at the well about true worship: "...Believe me, a time is coming when you will worship the Father neither on this mountain nor in Jerusalem...Yet a time is coming and has now come when the true worshipers will worship the Father in the Spirit and in truth, for they are the kind of worshipers the Father seeks. God is spirit, and his worshipers must worship in the Spirit and in truth" (John 4:21, 23).

DISCUSSION GUIDE: THIS IS GOD'S HOUSE

CHAPTER SUMMARY

God's dwelling place is not any particular building but the community of his people, the Church. This means we have access to him any place and any time, and he is with us in all places and at all times.

DISCUSSION QUESTIONS

1. Why did God dwell in a temple in the Old Testament?

2. How is the Church today God's house?

3. What is the appropriate way for a believer to act in a church building and how is that different from the way they act outside of one?

4. How can people maintain respect for the place people meet to worship without idolizing it?

5. What are some ways that we may unintentionally treat our everyday environment as less spiritual than a religious building or gathering?

I FEEL THE SPIRIT

It didn't matter what the sermon was about that week. I knew every week my pastor was going to find a way to say, "I feel the Spirit of God moving in here!" If I had a dollar for every time I've heard that in a church setting I'd finally be able to buy that Nintendo Switch I can't afford. I'd have far more money if I had a dollar for every time I heard a Christian complain that they *didn't* feel the Spirit of God moving in a particular church service. What concerns me most about these statements is not the statements themselves, there's nothing wrong with saying you feel or do not feel the Spirit's presence. What concerns me is what lies underneath these statements: the criteria used to judge whether or not the Holy Spirit is active in a particular place. In many cases, when people make judgments about the work of God's Spirit in a church, they do so with a flawed understanding of how the Holy Spirit really works. I know this because I used to say and think the same thing.

For example, when people say the Holy Spirit is moving in a particular place it's usually because of something they see or feel. I've heard people say they know the Holy Spirit is at work because they can sense a "change in the atmosphere." That's obviously not very specific. So, clearly, there must be something else that makes them feel that the atmosphere has changed. When I've asked what that is I've heard a number of answers. Some have said they could tell the Spirit was at work because they felt chills or goose bumps. Others have said they could tell the Spirit was active because they felt a certain emotion (maybe they found themselves crying or overwhelmed with excitement or joy). At other times people have claimed the Spirit was at work because the people were demonstrative: they stood up, they bowed, they lifted their hands, they shouted, they wept. According to many people, when these things are present they are proof that the Holy Spirit is at work. Which also means, of course, that when these things are not present the Holy Spirit is not at work.

This view of the Holy Spirit's work is very common. But there are problems with this common view. The first problem with these criteria is that they ignore the obvious influence of culture. I myself very much prefer demonstrative worship. Yet I know that whether or not a church stands, cries, shouts, and so forth is heavily influenced by the culture of the church and the cultural background of its members. Some churches regularly do all of these things because of cultural factors, and the Holy Spirit may not be responsible for any of it. Other churches rarely or never do these things because of cultural factors, yet the Holy Spirit may be at work in magnificent ways in their congregation. If we make these things the criteria by which we judge the Spirit's presence we will frequently be wrong. A second problem with these criteria is that they allow many false religions to qualify as communities where we can "feel the Spirit." Mormons, Muslims, Voodooists and others often experience these same feelings during their worship services. If we say that these things are the sign of the Holy Spirit's work we are saying that the Holy Spirit is more active in false religions than he is in many Christian churches. The Bible does not allow for that. The third problem is that the Holy Bible does not mention even one of these things as evidence of the Holy Spirit's work. Instead, the Scriptures offer us a criterion that is equally applicable to all cultures, inapplicable to other religions, and far more glorious than emotional feelings and physical actions.

According to the Bible, there are at least three things that show us when and where the Holy Spirit is at work. The first – and most important – is the proclamation of the gospel of Jesus Christ. Listen to Jesus' words in John 15:26, "When the Advocate comes, whom I will send to you from the Father—the Spirit of truth who goes out from the Father—he will testify about me." Where the Spirit is at work we will hear the truth about Jesus. Listen to Jesus again, this time in John 16:13-14, "But when he, the Spirit of truth, comes, he will guide you into all the truth. He will not speak on his own; he will speak only what he hears, and he will tell you what is yet to come. He will glorify me because it is from me that he will receive what he will make known to you." Again, we see that when the Holy Spirit is at work Jesus is glorified. Let's look at one last quote from Jesus about the work of the Holy Spirit. This one is found in Acts 1:8, "But you will receive power when the Holy Spirit comes on you; and you will be my witnesses in Jerusalem, and in all Judea and Samaria, and to the ends of the earth." In each passage Jesus makes it clear: when the Holy Spirit is at work we will hear the gospel of Jesus Christ proclaimed.

A second sign that the Holy Spirit is at work is what can be called regeneration or new birth. In John 3 Jesus explains to Nicodemus that one must be born again in order to be reconciled to God. When Nicodemus responds in confusion Jesus explains in verse 5, "Very truly I tell you, no one can enter the kingdom of God without being born of water and the

Spirit." The Spirit renews us, regenerates us, re-births us. We see this again in Titus 3:5 "He saved us through the washing of rebirth and renewal by the Holy Spirit." Where the Spirit is at work we will first see the gospel proclaimed and, second, we will see people reborn as they place their faith in Jesus Christ.

A third sign that the Holy Spirit is at work is that people are reflecting Jesus' character. Romans 8:13 says that the Holy Spirit empowers us to put our sinful behavior to death, "For if you live according to the sinful nature, you will die; but if by the Spirit you put to death the misdeeds of the body, you will live." But the Holy Spirit doesn't just put to death our evil thoughts and actions, He also produces righteous thoughts and actions. Galatians 5:22-23 reads, "...the fruit of the Spirit is love, joy, peace, patience, kindness, goodness, faithfulness, gentleness, and self-control."

There is nothing wrong with saying that the Holy Spirit is moving in this or that place. The problem is found in the criteria we often use to judge his activity. When judging the Holy Spirit's activity in a particular place we must be certain we are using the criteria provided in Scripture instead of the criteria learned from our experience. The Bible tells us we can be certain the Holy Spirit is at work when we hear the gospel proclaimed, when we see people place their faith in Jesus, and when we see these same people become more like Jesus in their character. By no means are these the only signs of the Spirit's work. But where the Spirit is at work we will *at least* see these things.

DISCUSSION GUIDE: I FEEL THE SPIRIT

Many of the common measurements we use to determine whether the Holy Spirit is present are unbiblical and inaccurate. Thankfully, the Bible provides us with very clear criteria that allow us to know for sure when the Holy Spirit is at work in our midst.

DISCUSSION QUESTIONS

1. What un-biblical (contrary to the Bible) or extra-biblical (not found in the Bible) criteria have you used in the past to determine if the Spirit is present and at work?

2. What are three biblical signs that the Holy Spirit is at work? Share a time that you have seen these evidences present in your church or in your life.

3. Describe ways in which you have seen a movement of the Spirit falsely or rightly attributed. What fruit (good or bad) has resulted?

4. How has the Holy Spirit changed your character to reflect Jesus'?

I HAVE PEACE ABOUT THIS DECISION

Life is filled with decisions. Sometimes making these decisions can be difficult, even frightening. This is especially true when there are several options that appear to be equally viable. In such cases we want God to tell us which decision we should make. But where the Scriptures are not explicit it can sometimes be difficult to discern which direction he is leading us. My pastor had a solution for that: simply make the decision you feel the most peace about. If you feel peace about a decision, he would say, then that is evidence that you are walking in God's will. If you don't feel peace, he would advise, that decision is not in line with the will of God.

I have since learned my pastor's view is not a unique one. Over the years I have heard Christian after Christian claim their decisions are in line with God's will with the simple words, "I have peace about this decision!" This idea that feeling peace about a decision is evidence that it is God's will (and that not feeling peace about a decision is evidence that it is not) is commonly held. Nevertheless, it is false.

First, we know it is false because it is nowhere taught in the Scriptures. Of course, there are many New Testament passages that promise peace to the believer. These passages, however, are not primarily concerned with an emotional feeling but with an objective fact. As the Apostle Paul explains in Romans 5:1, "Therefore, since we have been justified through faith, we have peace with God through our

Lord Jesus Christ." According to the Scriptures, believers experience objective peace as a result of being reconciled to God in Christ and not as a result of making the right decisions.

Second, we know it is false because we see multiple stories in the Bible that directly contradict it. For example, consider the story of Moses (Exodus 3:11 – 4:13). God spoke to Moses and made his will for Moses known. Yet Moses did not feel peace about the decision God was calling him to make. To the contrary, Moses was using every excuse he could find to get out of it! First he tried, "Who am I that I should go to Pharaoh?" When God didn't accept that excuse Moses tried a second: "Suppose they ask me who sent me? What should I tell them?" When that excuse didn't work Moses looked for another: "What if they do not believe me or listen to me?" When God refused that excuse Moses tried another: "But I have never been eloquent. I am slow in speech and tongue." Finally, with no plausible excuses remaining, Moses directly asked God for an out: "Pardon your servant, Lord. Please send someone else."

Does that sound like a man who feels peace about his decision? Of course not. Yet there is no question the decision he was making was entirely consistent with God's will. Not only did God communicate his will to Moses audibly, he also accompanied that verbal communication with multiple miracles. Yet even that was not enough to give Moses peace about the decision. This story, of course, is not unique to Moses. We find this with many of the Old Testament prophets. God clearly calls them to a specific task and they feel anything but peace about pursuing it.

The Bible also introduces us to characters who have the opposite experience. Take Jonah for example. As God's prophet, Jonah knew with certainty God had called him to go to Nineveh. Yet Jonah did not feel peace about that decision so he fled in the opposite direction. In doing so, Jonah was going directly against God's revealed will. If my pastor's claim was true then Jonah should not have been at peace with his decision. But he was. He was so at peace with his decision that he was able to sleep soundly on his getaway ship in the middle of a violent storm. While everyone else on the ship was concerned about their life, Jonah was peacefully sleeping below deck! Jonah knew precisely what God's will was. Yet he did not feel peace about making that decision. Instead, he felt peace as he fled — in willful rebellion — from the decision God told him to make.

Clearly, the claim that I can know I'm in God's will because "I have peace about that decision" does not find support in Scripture. Nevertheless, many Christians believe it. But we don't have to. The truth of the matter is we have been given everything we need to give us peace in our decisions: we have been given God's Word and we have been given God's Work.

God's Word often provides explicit instructions about what decisions we should and should not make and, even where it does not, it still supplies us with sufficient information to make a decision, confident that it is God's will. The Word does this by revealing to us who God is, what he is like, and what he wills. Like it did Moses, though, sometimes peace can evade us even when we know we're acting according to God's will.

Sometimes, it's even more complicated. There will be times when you have to apply God's Word to very specific situations in very specific ways and it will be unclear to you which of the two or three options before you is best. But this does not mean you need to look to your feelings to confirm God's will for you. Instead, you can look to God's Work. Specifically, you look to the work accomplished by Jesus Christ through his perfect life, sacrificial death, and victorious resurrection. It is through faith in this finished work that we can now be certain that "we have peace with God through our Lord Jesus Christ" (Romans 5:1). This means we can have peace in any decision that is consistent with God's Word because we know – through God's Work – that God will love us, be with us, and use our decision to make us more like his Son...no matter what decision we make.

But that's not all.

Here's the best part: Not only will God be with us when we make difficult decisions, he will also be with us when we make intentionally rebellious decisions that are explicitly contrary to what is prescribed in God's Word. Miraculously, even these do not disqualify us from peace. This is because peace ultimately has nothing to do with the decisions we make and everything to do with the decision God made to love sinners and adopt sinners as his own through the work of Jesus Christ. This is the source of all our peace, and the assurance we have that whether we make a wise decision, foolish decision, or even an outright rebellious decision, we are united to God because Jesus has made every decision perfectly in our place. And his work, he has promised us, is finished (John 19:30).

DISCUSSION GUIDE: I HAVE PEACE ABOUT THIS DECISION

CHAPTER SUMMARY
Feeling "peace" about a decision does not determine whether or not this decision is actually in line with the will of God. Instead, God guides us through his Word and his work.

DISCUSSION QUESTIONS

1. How does a believer experience true peace?

2. Have you ever made any decisions you felt at peace about that turned out to be the wrong choice? Have you ever made any decisions you did not feel peace about that later proved to be wise choices? Explain.

3. What is the best way to make a decision using the Bible as our guide?

4. In those decisions where the Bible does not provide a specific course, how does the gospel provide direction and encouragement?

GOD WANTS YOU TO BE RICH

No matter what text my pastor was preaching from on a given Sunday, the sermon would always include a promise of some coming blessing. "God wants you to prosper," he would say, "God wants to bless you," "God wants his kids to have the best." Whichever phrase he chose to use in any particular sermon we knew what he meant: "God wants you to be rich!"

I must confess I initially found this teaching very attractive. Can you blame me? Who wouldn't want to hear that the all-powerful Lord of the universe is personally committed to granting them all of their earthly desires for health, wealth, and prosperity? As inherently self-serving creatures we are drawn to this inherently self-serving message. This must be why so many Christians believe it (because there is certainly no other reason to do so). Unfortunately for its proponents, though the claim that "God wants you to be rich!" is popular, it is also an outright lie.

We know this teaching is a lie because the Scriptures contradict it. If it were true that the righteous should expect material prosperity then Jesus should have been the richest of all. But he wasn't. Instead, Jesus was born to poor parents (Luke 2:24) and, as an adult, had no place to lay his head (Luke 9:58). Whatever money Jesus had was equally shared with his disciples (John 12:6) while every material possession we see him using was borrowed from someone else. If Jesus were rich he would not have had to sail in a borrowed boat (Mark 3:9), pay his taxes with a borrowed coin (Matthew 17:27), ride on a borrowed donkey (Matthew 21:2), eat his Last Supper in a borrowed room (Matthew 26:18), and be buried in a borrowed tomb (Luke 23:50-53). Would God treat his own holy Son so shabbily if it were true that God promises that the righteous will receive material prosperity?

Lest we think that Jesus' experience was unique let us also consider the life of the Apostle Paul. As the author of most of the New Testament there is no question Paul was a faithful follower of Christ. He both figuratively and literally gave his life in service to God and God's people. If it is true that "God wants you to be rich!" then Paul should be the richest Christian of all. Speaking of himself and his fellow-apostles Paul writes, "To this very hour we go hungry and thirsty, we are in rags, we are brutally treated, we are homeless…We have become the scum of the earth, the garbage of the world — right up to this moment" (1 Corinthians 4:11, 13b).

As we review the life of Jesus and the life of Paul we see that God's Word does not teach that Christians should expect to experience worldly prosperity, but it does teach that Christians should expect to experience worldly suffering. As Paul himself explains, "…everyone who wants to live a godly life in Christ Jesus will be persecuted" (2 Timothy 3:12).

My pastor would ignore this clear teaching and try to draw our attention to other passages, which he believed supported his position that "God wants you to be rich!" For example, he would point to 3 John 2 as evidence that God wants you to "prosper in all things and be in health" (NKJV). What he failed to realize is that these words are not a promise from God but a prayer from John on behalf of a friend, not different from any similar prayer we might pray for those that we love.

The second Scripture my pastor would cite in defense of his teaching was Deuteronomy 28:3-6, which says, "You will be blessed in the city and blessed in the country. The fruit of your womb will be blessed, and the crops of your land and the young of your livestock... You will be blessed when you come in and blessed when you go out." Our church loved this promise so much that we even sang a "worship" song consisting of these words. The problem, though, is this Scripture does not actually say what my pastor taught us it said. He taught us this passage is God's promise to grant Christians material prosperity if they obey his commands. But it's not. This passage is one portion of a much longer passage wherein God is speaking (through Moses) to the nation of Israel about the unique covenant he has made with them as a nation. It was a conditional covenant (which Israel broke) detailing blessings for their obedience and curses for their disobedience. Thus, the promises of Deuteronomy 28 are not something we look forward to seeing fulfilled in contemporary Christians. They are promises that we look back upon as already fulfilled in ancient Israel's failure and in Jesus Christ's perfect obedience.

There is not a shred of Biblical evidence to support the popular claim that "God wants you to be rich!" Instead, there is a mountain of evidence that suggests this is the *last* thing Christians should expect. Of course, that is not to say there won't be Christians who experience material prosperity as a gift from God.

It is, however, to say that such people will be in the minority as there is no direct link between being a faithful Christian and being financially prosperous. This is why the Apostle Paul directly rebukes those who see a link between godliness and financial gain as "conceited" people who "understand nothing" (1 Timothy 6:4).

The mark of a faithful Christian is not material prosperity but godly contentment in any and every financial situation (see 1 Timothy 6:6, Philippians 4:11-13). This contentment is possible and reasonable because no matter their wealth, Christians are rich because they have been adopted by the God of all glory and thereby possess "an inheritance that can never perish, spoil, or fade" (1 Peter 1:4). Thus, Christians have no need for earthly riches because, as is so wonderfully stated in 2 Corinthians 8:9, "...you know the grace of our Lord Jesus Christ, that though he was [spiritually] rich, yet for your sake he became poor, so that you through his poverty might become [spiritually] rich." In this sense, God *does* want you to be rich and he has, in fact, *given you the riches!* Through faith in Jesus (given to you by God) you have also been given the incomparable spiritual riches of unity with the Triune God, the righteousness of Jesus Christ, the forgiveness of the Father, and the presence and power of God's Holy Spirit. As a Christian you are rich beyond belief — regardless of your financial situation — because you have freely received all of this and more "in accordance with the riches of God's grace that he lavished on us" (Ephesians 1:7-8).

DISCUSSION GUIDE: GOD WANTS YOU TO BE RICH

God does not promise to make the believer rich or prosper them materially in this world. Instead, God promises the believer something far more glorious.

DISCUSSION QUESTIONS

1. The idea that God wants his people to be wealthy tends to be most prevalent among the materially poor and the lower-middle class. Why do you think this is so?

2. Have you or anyone you know been a part of a church that preaches the "prosperity gospel"? How would you describe the material fruit of that church? How about the spiritual fruit?

3. Many people who reject the prosperity gospel tilt all the way to the other side of the spectrum to what is known as the poverty gospel (the teaching that God's true followers will be poor). What is the danger in this? What biblical evidence contradicts it?

4. In what ways has God promised to prosper the believer?

5. Besides giving generously, how else should a materially prosperous Christian use their resources to serve Jesus and his people?

THAT WILL MAKE YOU SIN

My pastor was always trying to keep me from sinning. On the surface that may not sound like a problem. But it was. The problem was not *that* he tried to keep me from sin but *how* he tried to keep me from sin. He tried to keep me from sin by keeping me from certain people, places, and things.

I once confided to one of my pastor's assistants that I was struggling to consistently obey God in several areas. This gracious woman heard my cry for help and responded by telling me how to overcome this struggle: "You listen to secular music," she said. "That's why you're still struggling with these things. If you get all of the secular CDs out of your house you'll be surprised at how quickly these struggles go away." The woman's advice was sincere and well-intentioned. It was also awful and unbiblical. When people point to music, movies, alcohol, places, or other people as the source of sin they train us to think that we can avoid evil by avoiding certain people or things. They train us to think that our sin is caused by something outside of us instead of inside of us. They mask the true cause of our problems.

The claim that "That will make you sin!" is based on a flawed view of humanity. Its mistake is in its claim that a person is basically morally neutral and that the choices they make in life determine their moral state: sinful or righteous.

The Bible clearly teaches that our sin is not caused by external forces but internal ones. James explains this well in his letter: "When tempted, no one should say,

'God is tempting me.' For God cannot be tempted by evil, nor does he tempt anyone; but *each of you is tempted when you are dragged away by your own evil desire and enticed*. Then, after desire has conceived, it gives birth to sin; and sin, when it is full-grown, gives birth to death" (1:13-15, emphasis mine). The thing that drags us away toward sin is not a pull from outside of us but a push from inside of us.

Of course Satan does use things outside of us to exploit the sinful desires inside of us. For this reason many of us should avoid certain music, certain movies, certain beverages, and certain places as a matter of wisdom. But this is not because of the power of these external things to make us sin. On the contrary, it is because of the power of the sin within us and its desire to misuse external things to feed its own lustful cravings. This is why Jesus warns,

> "Nothing outside you can define you by going into you. Rather, it is what comes out of you that defiles you...For from within, out of your hearts, come evil thoughts, sexual immorality, theft, murder, adultery, greed, malice, deceit, lewdness, envy slander, arrogance and folly. All these evils come from inside and defile you" (Mark 7:15, 20-23).

By itself this is very bad news. If our problem were external things our solution would be very simple. We could save ourselves by simply avoiding those external things. But external things are not our problem. The sinful cravings that dwell in the depths of our heart are our problem. And we are powerless to overcome them in our own power.

But there is good news.

The good news is that Jesus can and does save his people from the sinful cravings that dwell in their hearts. He does this, first, by regenerating us through his Holy Spirit. As he does so he fulfills God's ancient promise from Ezekiel 36:26-27, "I will give you a new heart and put a new spirit in you; I will remove from you your heart of stone and give you a heart of flesh. And I will put my Spirit in you and move you to follow my decrees and be careful to keep my laws." This gift of a new heart is accompanied by new desires and new power to love God above self and love righteousness above sin. A second way that Jesus saves us from the sinful cravings of our hearts is by eliminating the judgment our sinful nature merits. He did this by choosing to be judged in our place, bearing the full wrath of God both for our sinful desires and for our sinful actions. As a result, through faith in who Jesus is and what Jesus has done, we find freedom from the oppression of our heart's sinful cravings and, when our old cravings do rear their ugly head, we find freedom from the eternal consequences our cravings and actions deserve.

Every individual can and should feel free to avoid any external things he or she desires. But we dare not do so thinking that avoiding them will rescue us from evil or from God's wrath. Such rescue is found only in Jesus.

DISCUSSION GUIDE: THAT WILL MAKE YOU SIN

While culture may encourage us and even tempt us to sin, it is never the source of our sin. The source of our sin is actually internal. As such, escaping from certain aspects of culture (though at times wise) does not solve our sin problem since our sin problem resides in our heart.

DISCUSSION QUESTIONS

1. What area of the culture do you feel has the largest negative affect on you and why?

2. What does your answer to the above reveal about your heart? What can you do to in response?

3. Should there be any restrictions placed on where people go, what they listen to, and with whom they interact? If yes, where, who, and why?

4. Is there any danger in participating too much in the broader culture? If so, what and why?

5. If a Christian chooses to freely participate in the culture in the ways discussed in this chapter, how should they go about showing they are "not of this world"?

SPEAK IT INTO EXISTENCE

The person who shows every sign of being ill is told, "Don't claim that." The individual with a diagnosed disease is told to "claim healing." Poor people are encouraged to "speak prosperity" over their lives. In short, virtually anything you want can be yours so long as you "speak it in faith." Why? Because my pastor and others are convinced that Christians have the power to speak things into existence.

It may surprise you to hear that I don't have any problem at all with this concept of speaking things into existence…so long as it's God who is doing the speaking.

I have a tremendous problem with the idea that human beings have the power to speak things into existence. Those who teach that human beings can create reality by their words are responsible for the suffering of many as those who hear and follow this teaching are eventually left with only two options: to be disappointed with God for not supplying what they spoke or to be disappointed in themselves for not speaking it in faith. Either way, the lie has done its damage.

Speaking things into existence is so anti-biblical that even the passages that preachers use to defend the teaching actually prove the exact opposite. For example, in Genesis 1 we are introduced to God as he creates the entire universe out of nothing by speaking things into existence (as in "Let there be light" and "Let the land produce vegetation"). Some preachers want you to believe that this passage proves that words do create reality. But it doesn't. It proves that *God's* words create reality. God—and God alone—holds the power to speak things into existence. This point is made clearly and forcefully in Lamentations, with this cry: "Who can speak and have it happen if the Lord has not decreed it? Is it not from the mouth of the Most High that both calamities and good things come?" (3:37-38) In other words, you can speak all you want but if the Lord has not spoken it first it simply will not happen. Ever.

A second passage used to defend this false teaching is Mark 11:22-24. In this passage, Jesus tells his disciples, "Have faith in God...Truly I tell you, if you say to this mountain, 'Go, throw yourself into the sea,' and do not doubt in your heart but believe that what you say will happen, it will be done for you. Therefore I tell you, whatever you ask for in prayer, believe that you have received it, and it will be yours." This passage does not show that human beings have the power to change reality according to their speech. It shows that God has the power to change reality according to his will. The opening phrase of the passage shows that Jesus is not teaching us to have faith in ourselves, or in our words, but to have faith in God. His promise is not that you will receive whatever you speak but, rather, that you will receive "whatever you ask for in prayer." We know from the rest of Scripture that this is not a blanket promise that God will answer our every prayer by giving us what we want but is, instead, a promise that God will answer our prayer when they are in accordance with his will. As his closest friend John would later write, "This is the confidence we have in approaching God: that if we ask anything *according to his will*, he hears us" (1 John 5:14, emphasis mine).

Far from being taught in the Scriptures, "speaking things into existence" is explicitly *contradicted* in the Scriptures. James 4:13-16 warns,

> "Now listen, you who say, 'Today or tomorrow we will go to this or that city, spend a year there, carry on business and make money.' Why, you do not even know what will happen tomorrow. What is your life? You are a mist that appears for a little while and then vanishes. Instead, you ought to say, 'If it is the Lord's will, we will live and do this or that.' As it is, you boast in your arrogant schemes. All such boasting is evil."

In short, to speak as if you have knowledge of the future, much less control over it, is pure evil. Every detail of our lives, according to James, is subject to "the Lord's will," not our own.

The lie that we can speak things into existence is no different than the lie the Serpent told Eve. It tells us we can be like God. We can't. Regardless of what we say—or don't say—God's will prevails. Always. This should not frustrate us. It should comfort us. Because God's will is not only to bring himself his greatest glory but also to bring us our greatest good. He has done just that by providing everything we need through *his* Word, Jesus Christ, who has rescued us from sin, Satan, death, and eternal judgment. God has spoken something truly amazing into existence: our righteousness and salvation. Like the light that broke into the dark of nothingness, our righteousness comes directly from God, through Jesus Christ.

There is not a single need left for us to speak into existence, even if we could. God speaks all good things and, on account of his word, they exist. This is Good News indeed.

DISCUSSION GUIDE: SPEAK IT INTO EXISTENCE

CHAPTER SUMMARY
Human beings do not have the power to speak circumstances into existence. Our faith should be placed in God and his power, not in ourselves and the power of our words.

DISCUSSION QUESTIONS

1. What are some reasons you might want to speak something into existence? What does this reveal about your understanding of God and life?

2. Proverbs 18:21 is often used by Christians as evidence that we can speak things into existence. In light of this chapter and the revelation of Scripture, how would you explain the proper interpretation of Proverbs 18:21?

3. How does the role of prayer relate to the question of speaking into existence?

4. What would it look like for you to apply the truths of James 4:13-16 to your daily life? What, if anything, would change?

YOU'RE NOT FILLED WITH THE SPIRIT IF YOU DON'T SPEAK IN TONGUES

"If you don't speak in tongues you're not filled with the Holy Spirit." That's what my pastor used to say. And he said it often. He said it so often people just assumed it was true. Regrettably, this is a remarkably common story. Countless Christians believe "if you don't speak in tongues you're not filled with the Holy Spirit" simply because their favorite pastor, their favorite television evangelist, or their favorite denomination told them so.

This upsets me.

It upsets me both because it's not true and because I have seen this particular lie drive many people away from God. One man I know spent years repeatedly going to the altar praying God would cause him to speak in tongues. When the tongues never came he eventually left church altogether, assuming God did not want to save him since God would not fill him with the Holy Spirit. Another man came to worship with the people of God every time the doors to the church opened, but he refused to pursue involvement in ministry or to marry the Christian woman of his dreams because he wasn't yet "filled with the Holy Spirit" and was told he could not do either of those things until he showed he spoke in tongues. Just before I sat down to write this chapter I heard of another man who responded to an altar call at a local church. He came forward to publicly express his newfound faith in Jesus but was told he was not yet a Christian because he did not speak in tongues.

Stories like these are especially heartbreaking because there is no biblical evidence that supports this teaching. Of course, those who claim "you're not filled with the Holy Spirit if you don't speak in tongues" deny this and point to Acts 2 as their proof text. Yet even our brief review of Acts 2 will reveal that the chapter teaches no such thing.

The second chapter of Acts describes what may be called the beginning of the Church. Jesus has ascended into heaven and left his disciples with these instructions, "Do not leave Jerusalem, but wait for the gift my Father promised, which you have heard me speak about. For John baptized with water, but in a few days you will be baptized with the Holy Spirit" (Acts 1:4b-5). The disciples obeyed their Master and waited together in Jerusalem until, on the day of Pentecost, the promise arrived. Luke, the author of Acts, describes the event in Acts 2:1-4,

> "When the day of Pentecost came, they were all together in one place. Suddenly a sound like the blowing of a violent wind came from heaven and filled the whole house where they were sitting. They saw what seemed to be tongues of fire that separated and came to rest on each of them. All of them were filled with the Holy Spirit and began to speak in other tongues as the Spirit enabled them."

My pastor would point to this passage and say, "See, every one of them received the Holy Spirit and every one of them spoke in tongues. This obviously means that you are not filled with the Holy Spirit unless you speak in tongues." There are multiple problems with this conclusion. First, the remainder of Acts 2 reveals that as Jesus' disciples were speaking in tongues their audience heard them speaking in existing languages that they had never been trained to speak. If my pastor's conclusion is accurate then he himself is not a Christian because when he speaks in tongues his hearers do not here him speaking in existing languages as the disciples did in Acts 2. The second problem with my pastor's conclusion is that it makes the passage say something it was never intended to say.

One of the basic rules of biblical interpretation is to distinguish between descriptive passages and prescriptive passages. A descriptive passage is a passage that explains what happened at a certain time, in a certain place, with a certain group of people. Its purpose is to tell us about something that once happened rather than tell us about something that should always happen. A prescriptive passage, on the other hand, is a passage that explains what ought to be true of all Christians, in all places, at all times. Its purpose is to identify a particular belief, behavior, or characteristic that should mark every Christian. Acts 2 is not a prescriptive passage but a descriptive passage. Luke is providing us with a historical account of how the Church came into being at a specific point in time. Nowhere does he state or even imply that what the disciples experienced when the Church began is to be the normative experience as the Church expands.

This principle is so basic to biblical interpretation that even those who tell you that "you're not filled with the

Holy Spirit unless you speak in tongues" do not expect to see the other signs that are present in this passage. As we saw in Acts 2:1-4 above, the coming of the Holy Spirit was not only marked by tongues but also by the sound of a "violent wind" and images of "tongues of fire" resting upon each disciple. If someone points to Acts 2 to claim "you're not filled with the Holy Spirit unless you speak in tongues" they must also claim that you are not filled with the Spirit unless there is fire resting upon your head and the sound of a violent wind blowing through the building you are in.

It is inappropriate to take a descriptive text that explains what once happened and treat it like a prescriptive text that explains what should always happen. Instead, the wise Bible reader will interpret the descriptive text in light of all of the prescriptive texts that speak to the same issue. As we examine several such texts it will become clear that the experience of the disciples in Acts 2 was a unique experience intended to mark the Church's beginning and that as modern Christians are filled with the Holy Spirit they may or may not speak in tongues.

The first prescriptive text we will examine is 1 Corinthians 12:4-11,

> "There are different kinds of gifts, but the same Spirit distributes them. There are different kinds of service, but the same Lord. There are different kinds of working, but in all of them and in everyone it is the same God at work. Now to each one the manifestation of the Spirit is given for the common good. To one there is given through the Spirit a message of wisdom, to another a message of knowledge by means

of the same Spirit, to another faith by the same Spirit, to another gifts of healing by that one Spirit, to another miraculous powers, to another prophecy, to another distinguishing between spirits, to another speaking in different kinds of tongues, and to still another the interpretation of tongues. All these are the work of one and the same Spirit, *and he distributes them to each one, just as he determines*" (emphasis mine).

The Apostle Paul's point in this passage is clear: the Holy Spirit distributes different spiritual gifts to different people according to his own free choice. Thus, the Holy Spirit does give the gift of tongues to some people while giving different gifts to others. As Paul continues his argument in 1 Corinthians 12 he asks his audience a series of rhetorical questions in verses 29-30, "Are all apostles? Are all prophets? Are all teachers? Do all work miracles? Do all have gifts of healing? Do all speak in tongues? Do all interpret?" Paul does not answer his own questions because the implied answer is a plain "no." Consequently we should not expect that any one of these things will be present in any and all Spirit-filled people. According to Paul, there is only one gift that is universally present in all who are filled with the Holy Spirit. He mentions that gift earlier in this same chapter. In 1 Corinthians 12:3 he writes, "no one who is speaking by the Spirit of God says, 'Jesus be cursed,' and no one can say, 'Jesus is Lord,' except by the Holy Spirit." In other words, those who are filled with the Holy Spirit are not those who have been given the gift to speak in tongues but those who have been given the gift to worship Jesus as Lord.

This same point is made in another prescriptive text:

> "And you also were included in Christ when you heard the word of truth, the gospel of your salvation. When you believed, you were marked in him with a seal, the promised Holy Spirit" (Ephesians 1:13).

Here Paul explains that the Holy Spirit is given to God's people when they believe the gospel of Jesus Christ (not when they speak in tongues). It is noteworthy that Paul describes the Holy Spirit as "the promised Holy Spirit." In referring to the Holy Spirit in this way he is making a connection to Jesus' words to his disciples in Acts 1:8a, "you will receive power when the Holy Spirit comes upon you." By making this connection Paul is showing us that Jesus' promise is fulfilled when the Holy Spirit comes upon believers at their conversion and not when they speak in tongues.

There are a number of other prescriptive passages in Scripture that communicate this same truth but we have already examined enough of them to expose the claim that "you're not filled with the Holy Spirit if you don't speak in tongues" as the false teaching that it is. At this point it is appropriate to conclude our study with a passage that shows that the Holy Spirit is not only given upon conversion, he is also the cause of conversion:

> "[H]e saved us, not because of righteous things we had done, but because of his mercy. He saved us through the washing of rebirth and renewal by the Holy Spirit, whom he poured out on us generously through Jesus Christ our Savior, so that, having been justified by his

grace, we might become heirs having the hope of eternal life" (Titus 3:5-7).

The Holy Spirit is not given to us because we clean up our lives or because we tarry long enough in prayer. The Holy Spirit is given to us because of God's mercy, poured out freely on all whom Jesus saves. It is because of the free gift of the Holy Spirit that we had the desire and the power to say "yes" to Jesus to begin with, and continue to have the desire and the power to follow him every day after. Whether or not we ever speak in tongues, if our faith is in Jesus Christ, we presently possess the gift of the Holy Spirit because God presently possesses us.

DISCUSSION GUIDE: YOU'RE NOT FILLED WITH THE SPIRIT IF YOU DON'T SPEAK IN TONGUES

CHAPTER SUMMARY

The believer is filled with the Holy Spirit upon conversion. Speaking in tongues are one of many gifts of the Spirit, but the Spirit alone chooses who receives which gifts.

DISCUSSION QUESTIONS

1. What are some ways you can determine whether a passage of Scripture is descriptive or prescriptive?

2. 1 Corinthians 12:31 tells us to "eagerly desire the greater gifts." In the context of 1 Corinthians 12, what are those greater gifts? How should we as Christians express our eager desire for them?

3. The author argues that the believer receives the Holy Spirit at conversion. Why is it important we believe that? What theological and practical benefits

4. If speaking in tongues is not the biblical evidence that you're filled with the Holy Spirit then what is?

RECOMMENDED RESOURCE
Showing the Spirit: A Theological Exposition of 1 Corinthians 12-14 by D.A. Carson

THAT'S THE DEVIL

"That's the devil!"

Those three words were my pastor's explanation for any and every undesired occurrence in life.

You lost your job?

"That's the devil!"

You're feeling sick?

"That's the devil!"

You're tempted to sin?

"That's the devil!"

You were late for church?

"That's the devil!"

In this case he even cast out the demon of "tardiness" from everyone who arrived late to the service.

Since my pastor taught us to credit the devil for so much it was common to find the devil playing a central role in our worship services. We preached about him, we talked about him, and we talked to him ("Satan, the Lord rebuke you!"). On some weeks we would go so far as to sing songs to him ("I command you Satan/in the name of the Lord/to drop your weapons and flee!"). I must admit that I found all of this exciting at the time. Having an enemy to wage war against always gets the blood pumping. But, as exciting as it was, it was often based on a lie.

That is not to say the devil does not exist – he does. That is also not to say that the devil is not actively working against Christians – he most certainly is. We know these things because the Scriptures testify that our "enemy the devil prowls around like a roaring lion looking for someone to devour" (1 Peter 5:8) and because more than 20 New Testament books mention our battle with Satan. Thus, my pastor's lie was not that the devil was aiming to destroy us – this is his constant aim. My pastor's lie was that the devil was the primary cause of *everything* undesirable in our lives. This is a lie because, in the Bible, God is credited for many such things that we often attribute to the devil.

While we obviously cannot exhaust every possible issue here we can look at several examples where the Bible credits God for things that Christians tend to blame on the devil.

First, let us examine the issue of poverty. When Christians face financial challenges they often claim "that's the devil." But, in his Word, God himself takes credit for poverty just as he does for prosperity. 1 Samuel 2:7 reveals, "The Lord sends poverty and wealth; he humbles and he exalts."

Physical illness is a second issue that the devil often receives the sole credit for. But the Bible testifies that while demonic forces may often be involved in sickness (Matthew 17:14-18, 2 Corinthians 12:7) God himself may also be involved. 2 Kings 15:5 tells us that "The Lord afflicted the king with leprosy" and 2

Chronicles 21:18a explains that "the Lord afflicted Jehoram with an incurable disease." These straightforward statements should not surprise us. This is precisely what God promised would happen to the people of Israel if they failed to keep the covenant. In Deuteronomy 28:21-22a we read, "The Lord will plague you with diseases until he has destroyed you from the land you are entering to possess. The Lord will strike you with wasting disease, with fever and inflammation..."

A third (and related) problem the devil is often blamed for is death. But God himself claims to have authority over death just as he has authority over life. "I put to death and I bring to life," he says in Deuteronomy 32:39. Thus, it is not the devil who determines when people die, but God. As Job rightly assesses, "The days of mortals are determined; you have decreed the number of their months and have set limits they cannot exceed" (Job 14:5).

Therefore,, though the devil is *often* maliciously active in the events in our lives, he does not get to determine the events of our lives. God does. This is true of poverty, physical illness, and death, as we saw above. It is also true of barrenness (1 Samuel 1:6), confusion (Deuteronomy 28:20), and war (Judges 9:23). It is, in fact, true of everything both good and bad. The prophet Jeremiah asks rhetorically, "Who can speak and have it happen if the Lord has not decreed it? Is it not from the mouth of the Most High that both calamities and good things come?" (Lamentations 3:37-38).

This is why we cannot look at the "negative" pieces of our lives and simply conclude, "That's the devil!" We cannot do this, first, because it is not the devil but God who is ultimately in control of all things. If and when the devil is involved in our suffering he is only involved as an agent who, even in his rebellion against God, is unintentionally doing God's will. Second, we cannot do this because the things we perceive as negative are sometimes the things that are actually the most glorifying to God and the most good for us.

We see both of these facts illustrated in the life of Job. During the course of Job's story we find him losing his money, his children, his health, and his friends. Yet it was God, and not Satan, who first mentioned Job as a potential "target" for the devil (Job 1:8). Then it was God, and not Satan, who determined exactly what the devil could and could not do to Job (Job 1:12, 2:6). It is clear from Job 1 and 2 that Satan was *pleased* to play an active role in Job's suffering. But it is also exceedingly clear that he was only able to do so because God told him to. And while we do not know the exact reason why God chose to use the devil to bring this suffering into Job's life, we do know that it was both for Job's good and for God's glory. Even Job recognizes this and says to God, "My ears had heard of you but now my eyes have seen you. Therefore I despise myself and repent in dust and ashes" (Job 42:5-6).

Perhaps the most illuminating picture of how God uses the evil of the devil to accomplish his own good purposes is found in Jesus' death. Jesus was and is the only truly innocent person to ever live, yet he died the painful and shameful death of a criminal. Satan was, of course, happy to play a lead role in this injustice. We are told that "Satan entered Judas" before he went to betray Jesus to the chief priests

(Luke 22:3). Yet, even as Satan was acting out of his hatred for God, he was actually doing God's will. For the Bible explains "it was the Lord's will to crush him" (Isaiah 53:10) according to his own "deliberate plan and foreknowledge" (Acts 2:23). What appeared to be Satan's victory was actually his defeat as the worst suffering in human history brought God his greatest glory and brought us our greatest good (Colossians 2:15).

The devil may or may not be directly involved in the pieces of your life you perceive as negative. Either way, he is committed to destroying you. Ironically, one of the ways he might like to destroy you is by convincing you to set your focus on him rather than on your Lord. Rather than giving him this pleasure, though, you can actively fight against him and his works by setting your sights on Jesus who reigns victorious over the devil and masterfully uses the devil's rebellion for his own good purposes. "For in him [Jesus] all things were created: things in heaven and on earth, visible and invisible, whether thrones or powers or rulers or authorities; all things have been created through him and for him" (Colossians 1:16).

DISCUSSION GUIDE: THAT'S THE DEVIL

CHAPTER SUMMARY
Though the devil hates us and is actively at work against us, not every negative occurrence in our lives can be attributed to the Devil; God is often working to use the painful aspects of life for His glory.

DISCUSSION QUESTIONS
1. How does blaming the devil for everything free people from personal responsibility?

2. In what ways does blaming the devil for everything reduce our view of God?

3. As we see with Job, the negative occurrences in our lives can often be used to give God glory and bring us good. Describe a time where God use something in your life that appeared to be negative to bring him glory and/or bring you good.

4. Is there any way we can discern whether an attack is from the devil or orchestrated by God? What are some biblical teachings that might help us answer this question?

5. How might your response to a "negative" situation be different if you believe God is behind it instead of the devil? How might your response be different if you are confident it is an attack of the devil?

RECOMMENDED RESOURCE
Spiritual Warfare: Christians, Demonization & Deliverance by Dr. Karl Payne

GOD HEALS ALL WHO HAVE FAITH

Americans in general are uncomfortable with sickness and disease. Nowhere was this truer than in the church I used to be a part of. Sick people were not just considered to be physically ill, they were considered to be spiritually ill. My pastor taught us that God wanted all of his people to be healed of sickness and disease and that this healing was freely available to any and every Christian who asked for it in faith. If a Christian did not receive the healing they asked for it was a sign that their faith was lacking because, as my pastor often said, "God heals all who have faith!"

This teaching has harmed countless people in my church and others. It has led some to despair because they see their continued sickness as proof of their own inability to have enough faith. It has led others to turn from God because they see their continued sickness as proof that he cannot be trusted to do what he promises. It has even led many to death because they thought that to pursue medical help would be to reveal a lack of faith in God. What makes these stories especially tragic is that they are all based on a lie. The claim that "God heals all who have faith" both contradicts human experience and contradicts God's Word.

If God truly promised healing to all who believe, then we should expect to see a large number of believers living forever. We do not see that, of course, because every person eventually dies – most often of sickness and disease. Even those whom Jesus raised from the dead ultimately died with their contemporaries, just like everyone else. Thousands of years of human experience confirm that the human death rate is 100% and that faithful believers are not an exception to the rule. From this evidence alone we can conclude that while God can and does temporarily heal some he does not permanently heal anyone while in this world.

This is also the plain teaching of the Bible, our most trustworthy source of evidence. In the life of the Apostle Paul alone there are at least four instances that directly contradict the claim that "God heals all who have faith." The first instance is found in Acts 28:1-10. In these verses Luke tells us of Paul's experience on the island of Malta. During his time there the father of the island's chief official was ill. Paul prayed for him and healed him of his fever and dysentery. "When this had happened," we read in verse 9, "the rest of the sick on the island came and were cured." Though some point to this verse to prove his claim that "God heals all who have faith" this verse actually disproves that claim because Luke does not give us any reason to believe that these people worshiped Jesus as God. Instead, they thought that Paul himself was a god (Acts 28:6). This tells us that while God may physically heal some people this healing is not the guaranteed consequence of their faith but the consequence of his own sovereign choosing. In this case God chose to heal people who did not have faith in him, in the three cases that follow he chose not to heal those who did have faith in him.

The first of these cases is Paul's fellow-laborer in the gospel, Trophimus. In concluding his second letter to Timothy Paul notes, "I left Trophimus sick in Miletus" (2 Timothy 4:20). Though God had previously given

Paul the ability to heal the unbelieving sick at Malta he chose not to give him the ability to heal the faithful Trophimus.

The second of these cases is Paul's son in the gospel, Timothy. In his first letter to Timothy Paul exhorts the young pastor to, "Stop drinking only water, and use a little wine because of your stomach and your frequent illnesses" (1 Timothy 5:23). If Paul believed that "God heals all who have faith" he would have offered faithful prayer as the solution to Timothy's frequent illnesses instead of wine. The fact that he did not is evidence that Paul did not believe that healing was guaranteed to those who have faith.

The third case of God choosing not to heal one of his faithful is the case of Paul himself. In 2 Corinthians 12:7-9 Paul explains, "Therefore, in order to keep me from becoming conceited, I was given a thorn in my flesh, a messenger of Satan, to torment me. Three times I pleaded with the Lord to take it away from me. But he said to me, 'My grace is sufficient for you, for my power is made perfect in weakness.' Therefore I will boast all the more gladly about my weaknesses, so that Christ's power may rest on me." Though Paul does not tell us precisely what his issue was he does tell us that it was something that caused him physical pain in his physical body ("a thorn in my flesh"), resulting in weakness ("I will boast all the more gladly about my weaknesses"). Whatever Paul's particular ailment was, he asked the Lord to heal him of it on three different occasions. God eventually answered and told Paul that he would not heal him. My pastor would like you to believe that God chose not to heal Paul because Paul lacked faith. But that's not the reason that God gives to Paul. God tells Paul that it is for his own glory and for Paul's good that he will not heal him. It is difficult to imagine a more direct contradiction to the claim that "God heals all who have faith."

In spite of this overwhelming evidence many still argue that the Bible teaches "God heals all who have faith." To support this claim they point to the following passages:

> "But he was pierced for our transgressions, he was crushed for our iniquities; the punishment that brought us peace was on him, and *by his wounds we are healed*" *(emphasis mine)* – Isaiah 53:5.

> "'He himself bore our sins' in his body on the cross, so that we might die to sins and live for righteousness; '*by his wounds you have been healed*'" *(emphasis mine)* – 1 Peter 2:24.

My pastor asserts that these verses reveal that Jesus' death on the cross secured physical healing for his people. While it is clear from these scriptures that Jesus' death does provide healing there is no reason to believe that this healing is physical. In both of these passages the focus is plainly on spiritual sickness and not on physical sickness.

This is clear in the Isaiah passage as the prophet tells us that Jesus will be pierced for our transgressions, crushed for our inequities and punished to bring us peace. All three of these accomplishments speak to our spiritual sickness. Isaiah explains that Jesus was punished for our sins (our "transgressions" and "iniquities") in order to rescue us from the consequence of our sin, which is our enmity with God (he "brought us peace"). When he adds that "by his wounds we are healed" he is not suddenly changing the subject from spiritual sickness to physical sickness. Instead, he is stating in a fourth way what he has already stated in three ways: that Jesus' death is the solution to our spiritual problem of sin.

The same is true in the verse quoted from 1 Peter above. Again, the context reveals that the author is concerned with our spiritual sickness, not with any physical sickness. Speaking of Jesus' atonement Peter writes that Jesus bore our sins "*so that* we might die to sins and live for righteousness" (emphasis mine). Peter's point is that the purpose of Jesus' death was to solve our spiritual problem of sin. When Peter then adds "by his wounds you have been healed" he is not changing his point, he is reinforcing it, which is why he continues to speak of the spiritual fruit of Jesus' death in the very next verse, "For 'you were like sheep going astray,' but now you have returned to the Shepherd and Overseer of your souls" (1 Peter 2:25).

In trying to make these passages speak of a temporary physical healing people have drawn attention away from the far more glorious gift of permanent spiritual healing, which is the primary emphasis of these passages. This is both unfortunate and unnecessary. It is unfortunate because it robs Jesus of his full glory. It is unnecessary because if we properly emphasize that Jesus cured our spiritual sickness on the cross we will recognize that, in so doing, Jesus also cured all the symptoms of our spiritual sickness, two of which are sickness and death. This is not a guarantee that those who are in

Christ will be presently and temporarily free from physical sickness. It is a far more magnificent guarantee that while they may suffer now those who are in Christ will be permanently free from physical sickness and physical death when Jesus raises them from the dead in glory. As Paul explained, in his weakness, "So will it be with the resurrection of the dead. The body that is sown is perishable, it is raised imperishable; it is sown in dishonor, it is raised in glory; it is sown in weakness, it is raised in power; it is sown a natural body, it is raised a spiritual body" (1 Corinthians 15:42-44a).

DISCUSSION GUIDE: GOD HEALS ALL WHO HAVE FAITH

CHAPTER SUMMARY
The claim that God will heal all people who have faith of all health problems is both unbiblical and very dangerous. The good news is that Jesus Christ's death on the cross does guarantee the healing we need most of all: healing from the sickness of sin and death.

DISCUSSION QUESTIONS

1. Have you or someone you know ever been hurt by the teaching that God heals all who have faith? Share your story.

2. Many people believe in the Lord's Prayer when Jesus says "On earth as it is in heaven" this is a promise of healing. The rationalization of this is there is no sickness in heaven and therefore if the believer prayed as Jesus prayed then they should be healed. Is this what Jesus meant? How do life and scripture contradict this? What is the danger, if any, behind this belief?

3. Has there been an occasion in your life where you asked God to heal someone and he has? An occasion where he has not? In either situation, how did you feel? Looking back on

those feelings, what do they say about the way you view(ed) God?

4. If God's choosing to heal people is his sovereign choice then is there any point to praying for healing at all? Why or why not?

5. Isaiah 53 is a prophecy of Jesus' great and mighty work that healed us of spiritual sickness. Pastor Cole writes that one of the implications of this is healing from the diseases of sickness and death. What other implications are there in this great work?

YOU HAVE A GENERATIONAL CURSE

My pastor had a very simple way to diagnose the root cause of every sin issue in the congregation. He simply attributed everything to a generational curse.

You have an eating disorder?

"That's because you have a generational curse!"

You had a child out of wedlock?

"That's because you have a generational curse!"

You struggle with lust or addiction?

"That's because you have a generational curse!"

My pastor blamed generational curses for every sin imaginable. If you were sinning in a particular way you were doing so because your parent or grandparent sinned in the same way. Whether you were a Christian or not was irrelevant; you had no choice but to sin in just the same way as they sinned.

In promoting this popular understanding of generational curses many will point to several passages in the Old Testament where God states that the sin of one man will impact his future descendants. One example of this is found in Numbers 14:18, "The Lord is slow to anger, abounding in love and forgiving sin and rebellion. Yet he does not leave the guilty unpunished; he punishes the children for the sin of the parents to the third and fourth generation." While this clearly teaches that our sin affects those who come after us, it does not teach "generational curses" in the way my pastor and many others claim.

Notice, first, that the passage says nothing about the cause of our sin, only the consequences. God does not say children will *sin* because of their parents' sin, he says children will be *punished* because of their parents' sin. Also, the very fact God promises to "not leave the guilty unpunished" implies that those who sin do so because of their own brokenness. This is why they are "the guilty." They are bound to sin, but not in a specific way because of the specific sins of their family.

Second, this verse does not state that believing children will be cursed for their parents' wickedness. In fact, it says those who turn to God in faith will experience God's forgiveness, not God's punishment, because God is "slow to anger, abounding in love and forgiving sin and rebellion." This is made plain in the verses that immediately follow Numbers 14:18. In verse 19 Moses asks God to "forgive the sin of these people, just as you have pardoned them from the time they left Egypt until now." Then, in verse 20, the Lord replied, "I have forgiven them, as you asked."

Third, there are other passages in Scripture where God explicitly states that repentant children will not share the guilt of their parents. The most exhaustive of these passages is Ezekiel 18. In Ezekiel 18:14-18 God declares that the repentant son will not be punished for his father's wickedness,

> "But suppose this son has a son who sees all the sins his father commits, and though he sees them, he does not do such things...He will not die for his father's sin; he will surely live. But his father will die for his own sin, because he practiced extortion, robbed his brother and did what was wrong among his people."

At this point God anticipates the objections of the Israelites who expect the son of a wicked man to inherit some sort of generational curse. God responds in verses 19-20,

> "Yet you ask, 'Why does the son not share the guilt of his father?' Since the son has done what is just and right and has been careful to keep all my decrees, he will surely live. The one who sins is the one who will die. The child will not share the guilt of the parent, nor will the parent share the guilt of the child. The righteousness of the righteous will be credited to them, and the wickedness of the wicked will be charged against them."

Though the sins of our ancestors certainly impact us in various ways, including spiritually, we can see that we have no reason to believe that a Christian is *bound* to sin a certain way because his relatives sin(ned) a certain way. Of course, we *used to* be bound in this way. When Adam sinned, all of his descendants inherited his sinful disposition so that every human being born since has been born a God-hater, enslaved by sin, and under God's wrath (Romans

5:12). In this sense, then, all of us have been under a generational curse.

The good news of the gospel is that God does not leave us to break this generational curse ourselves, which we are utterly powerless to do. Instead, God has broken this curse for us by becoming the curse for us in Jesus Christ. Galatians 3:13-14 announces that, "Christ redeemed us from the curse of the law by becoming a curse for us, for it is written: 'Cursed is everyone who is hung on a pole.' He redeemed us in order that the blessing given to Abraham might come to the Gentiles through Christ Jesus, so that by faith we might receive the promise of the Spirit."

In just these two verses sit three magnificent truths.

1. Jesus became cursed in our place. Though sinless in every way, he willingly became the one enslaved by sin and its judgment as our substitute. The generational curse we inherited from Adam was placed upon Jesus.
2. Jesus did this in order to free us from the curse we inherited. Those who belong to him are no longer bound to sin nor bound to be judged for sin.
3. The blessings promised to Abraham have come to us through Jesus Christ. This means we are now children of Abraham by faith, sealed by God's Holy Spirit. Thus, we have a new family — God's family — through which we have inherited blessings rather than a curse.

Christians need not live in fear of being incapable of escaping the clutches of sin because of a generational curse. Thanks to the gospel, the worst curse of all has been lifted forever. We are now freed to live in the confidence provided by the generational blessings we possess in Jesus Christ. Through faith in who he is and what he has done, God treats us as if we have lived as Jesus lived, obeyed as Jesus obeyed, and worshiped as Jesus worshiped. Thus, even if our parents were slaves to the worst of sins, we have been given the life of God's own Son as our own.

DISCUSSION GUIDE: YOU HAVE A GENERATIONAL CURSE

CHAPTER SUMMARY
The Bible does teach that humans are vulnerable to a generational curse, but not in the way that is often taught. The root of our sin is not in our parents but in the Original sin of Adam and we can be freed from its curse through Jesus' work.

DISCUSSION QUESTIONS

1. Our parents' sins are not the cause of our sins but can be an influence. In what ways have the sins of your parents influenced sin patterns in your life?

2. Have you ever felt trapped in the sin patterns of your parents? If so, in what ways can the gospel encourage you in the midst of those feelings?

3. What are some sin patterns in your parents' lives that you have seen Jesus rescue you from? What does this reveal about the power of the cross in your life?

4. What are some sin patterns in your life you do not want to influence your current or future children with? What can you do to protect them?

5. From Adam we inherited broken relationships with God, each other, and all of creation. In Christ all of these relationships are being restored. Share an example of how you have experienced restoration through Christ in one of these relational categories.

SHE'S NOT ANOINTED

My pastor was a self-proclaimed expert at determining who was and who was not anointed. And he did everything he could to make his judgments known. On more than one occasion he stood up before the entire congregation to complain about the woman who just led the church in songs of worship. "There was no anointing there!" he'd announce, shamelessly, as if the insulted woman could not hear him belittling her. "Now I have to bring in the anointing!" Needless to say, this caused significant pain for the young woman who led these songs at her pastor's request. But she was not the only one harmed by such statements. The damage from statements like these stretches to any and all who believe the lie that some Christians are anointed, some are not, and some people can tell the difference.

Many in the Church talk about anointing as though it were some sort of mystical power that God reserves for a certain class of Christians. They tell us there are different anointings that serve different functions. Some people are anointed to sing. Some are anointed to preach. Some have an anointing to pray or to counsel. My pastor used to go so far as to say that his wife was "anointed to shop." It seems as though there's an anointing for everything! But how do you get this anointing? Well, many people will tell you that you have to earn it. If you want to be anointed you need to pray, and fast, and give, and serve faithfully. Then, and only then, will God grant you this mysterious and mystical power.

I must admit that this perspective on the anointing is, in some ways, an attractive one. Who wouldn't want God to reward them for their obedience by setting them apart from others with a special and unique power? Yet as common as it is and as attractive as it is it is also utterly flawed. The way the Bible speaks about the anointing could not be more different.

In the Old Testament the word "anointing" is not used to describe some sort of mystical empowerment one must earn. Rather, it is used to describe the act of God setting apart a particular person for a particular position or a particular task. This anointing is given freely to those whom God chooses according to his own good pleasure. For instance, it pleased God to anoint Aaron as priest, David as king and Elisha as prophet, though they had done nothing to merit such positions. As these men were anointed spiritually (by God's action) they were subsequently anointed physically (by man's action) as oil was applied to their heads in ritualistic fashion.

In the New Testament this concept of anointing finds its ultimate fulfillment in Jesus Christ. The title "Christ" literally means "The Anointed One." To say that Jesus is The Anointed One is not to say he has received some mystical empowerment to preach, sing, pray, or shop better than his contemporaries. It is to say he has been uniquely set apart by God to "proclaim good news to the poor...freedom for the prisoners and recovery of sight to the blind, to set the oppressed free, to proclaim the year of the Lord's favor" (Luke 4:18-19).

Jesus is The Anointed One – he is the true and perfect prophet, the true and perfect priest, the true and perfect king. Does this mean that no one else can be anointed? No. In fact, it means the exact opposite. In the Old Testament only prophets, priests, and kings were anointed. In many of our modern churches only those who can do something exceptionally well on stage are considered to be anointed. But in the New Testament – because Jesus lived, died, and rose again – the anointing is no longer reserved for a special class of people. Now anyone and everyone who places their faith in Jesus is anointed simply by virtue of being united to The Anointed One.

The New Testament does not teach there are multiple anointings that are given to a certain class of Christians. The New Testament teaches there is one anointing and this anointing is given to every true Christian. This anointing is not a mystical power. This anointing is not a special skill. This anointing is a person – the Holy Spirit – who dwells in all who are in Christ to set them apart as God's special possession. This is made clear in 2 Corinthians 1:21-22 as the Apostle Paul explains, "…it is God who makes both us and you stand firm in Christ. He anointed us, set his seal of ownership on us, and put his Spirit in our hearts as a deposit, guaranteeing what is to come." The Apostle John agrees as he describes the anointing by using the same terms that Jesus uses to describe the Holy Spirit in John 14-16, "But you have an anointing from the Holy One, and all of you know the truth… As for you, the anointing you received from him remains in you, and you do not need anyone to teach you. But as his anointing teaches you about all things and as that anointing is real, not counterfeit— just as it has taught you, remain in him" (1 John 2:20, 27).

This means that the woman who sings powerfully and moves crowds to tears and goose bumps may not be anointed, while the woman who sings terribly and moves crowds to plug their ears may very well be. The difference between the anointed and the unanointed is not talent, skill, power, or righteous actions. The difference between the anointed and the unanointed is faith in Jesus Christ. The good news is that this means every single Christian is equally anointed by God. The bad news is that many Christians do not know this because they have heard the same lie I did.

DISCUSSION GUIDE: SHE'S NOT ANOINTED

CHAPTER SUMMARY
To be anointed is not to have an exceptional skill within you. To be anointed is to have an exceptional person within you, the Holy Spirit. Thus, all true Christians are anointed.

DISCUSSION QUESTIONS

1. What are the most common ways you have heard the term "anointing" used in Christian circles. Would you say you have mostly heard this word used properly? Or improperly? Why?

2. What are ways the anointing of the Holy Spirit manifests itself in the life of a believer?

3. What are the dangers of labeling some Christians as "anointed" at not others?

4. What are the benefits of being anointed by/with Holy Spirit?

JUST BELIEVE GOD

Just believe God.

That's my old pastor's formula for success in any area. You want your health to improve? *Just believe God.* You want your marriage to heal? *Just believe God.* You want to have more money? *Just believe God.* Whatever it is that you desire my pastor will tell you that you can have it if you *just believe God.* Have enough faith, and your wishes will be granted.

This teaching appeals to us for two obvious reasons. It appeals to us because it serves our fleshly desires. It tells us that we can have whatever we want whenever we want it. It also appeals to us because it serves our fleshly desires while *appearing* to be spiritual. It tells us the key to getting what we want is our faith in God. Because this teaching is so appealing we want to believe it. But we shouldn't.

The Bible does not teach that faith is some sort of spiritual credit card we can use to get God to do what we want him to do. Instead, it teaches that in all cases and at all times God does what *he* wants to do. As he says through his prophet Isaiah, "My purpose will stand, and I will do all that I please" (Isaiah 46:10). The psalmists echo this truth, proclaiming that God does "whatever pleases him" (Psalm 115:3, 135:6). Even the pagan king Nebuchadnezzar recognized that the most powerful human beings have zero control over God and what he does, saying, "All the peoples of the earth are regarded as nothing. He does as he pleases with the powers of heaven and the peoples of the earth. No one can hold back his hand or say to him: 'What have you done?'" (Daniel 4:35).

While we human beings are free to have and express our desires, we must acknowledge, like Nebuchadnezzar, that our desires are subject to God's will. Consider Proverbs 19:21: "Many are the plans in a human heart, but it is the Lord's purpose that prevails." James makes a similar point when writing to a community of faithful Christians who "believe God." He writes, "Now listen, you who say, 'Today or tomorrow we will go to this or that city, spend a year there, carry on business and make money.' Why, you do not even know what will happen tomorrow. What is your life? You are a mist that appears for a little while and then vanishes. Instead, you ought to say, 'If it is the Lord's will, we will live and do this or that'" (James 4:13-15).

This is not to say that God is not interested in giving us what we want. God is our loving Father who takes great pleasure in giving his children things that please them. Yet our faith never forces God to give us what he does not already will to give us. Whatever God gives us he gives us primarily because he desires to give it, not primarily because we desire to receive it. The Apostle John explains, "This is the confidence we have in approaching God: that if we ask anything according to his will, he hears us. And if we know that he hears us—whatever we ask—we know that we have what we asked of him" (1 John 5:14-15). The key phrase here is "according to his will." God does not give us what we want every time that we pray. He gives us what we want when we pray *in faith* according to his will.

The advice to "just believe God" is foolish because God always does what he wants, whether we believe him or not. It is also foolish because it teaches us to "just believe God" for things he has not promised us. To illustrate, a certain single man in my church may believe that Beyoncé will be faithful to him in sickness and in health, in good times and in bad, until death do them part. But the depth of his faith on this matter wouldn't impress you, it would concern you. Why? Because you know it is not wise to trust someone to do something that they never said they would do. That's not faith. That's presumption.

True faith is always a response to something that has been revealed; true faith is trusting someone to be who they said they would be or do what they said they would do. This is especially true of faith in God. We see this in Hebrews 11, where faith is discussed at great length. This chapter of the Bible has often been called "The Hall of Faith" because it includes brief profiles of those with exemplary faith. A review of this list reveals that these heroes of the faith are not being celebrated for simply "believing God" but for believing God would do what he promised. For example, Noah built the ark because he believed God was going to send a flood and save Noah, just as he said he would (Hebrews 11:7). Abraham left his homeland to go to a land he did not know because he believed God was going to give him the Promised Land, just as he said he would (Hebrews 11:8-10). Sarah gave birth to Isaac when she was far past childbearing age because she "considered him faithful who had made the promise" (Hebrews 11:11). As the author of Hebrews continues this line of thought he speaks of Isaac, Jacob, Joseph, Moses and others, in each case reminding us that true faith is trusting God to be who he said he would be and do what he said he would do. This is the type of faith that we are called to imitate.

We can follow my pastor's advice and "believe God" for better health, better jobs, more money, a new Lexus, and the perfect spouse, but if we do so we are not exercising faith. We are arrogantly trying to manipulate God to do our bidding and foolishly expecting him to do things he has never promised to do. This will inevitably lead to frustration and disappointment when God does not do what we have presumptuously believed he will do. Christian faith is simply trusting God to be who he said he will be and do what he said he will do. We trust him to save us from his wrath through Jesus Christ, conform us into the image of his Son, work all things out for our ultimate good, and never leave us nor forsake us. These things he has done. We can say with the Apostle Paul, "I know whom I have believed, and am convinced that he is able to guard what I have entrusted to him until that day" (2 Timothy 1:12). This faith is a miracle, allowing us to be content in any and every situation knowing that even when our health, relationships and finances fail us, the God who loves us never will.

DISCUSSION GUIDE: JUST BELIEVE GOD

CHAPTER SUMMARY
True faith does not believe God to do things he has not promised to do or to be someone he has not revealed himself to be. True faith believes in God for who He is, what He has done, and what He said He would do.

DISCUSSION QUESTIONS

1. The author writes, "true faith is trusting God to be who he said he would be and do what he said he would do. This is the type of faith that we are called to imitate." What is something God has promised you as a believer and how do you live in light of that promise?

2. Believers are most often told to "just believe God" when facing suffering. What are some things God has promised that we can and should believe God for in the midst of suffering?

3. Have you ever "believed God" for something he did not promise? If you did not get the thing you were waiting for, how did that make you feel towards God? Do you think your feelings were justified? Why or why not?

4. If you could have God give you anything you wanted what would it be? What does this reveal about your heart towards God and others?

5. Is "just believing God" always enough? Are there any specific promises in Scripture that require you put your belief into action?

DOCTRINE IS DANGEROUS

My pastor was against a lot of things (and even a lot of people). But it seemed that one enemy stood out among them all: theological doctrine. My pastor took advantage of every opportunity to speak against theological doctrine and those who chose to value it. Seminaries were "cemeteries" and those who dared to challenge false teaching were "heresy hunters." The overall picture he painted of those who took an interest in learning theology was that they were prideful, spiritually dry people who had a faith of the mind but not a faith of the heart. He often summarized his position with the simple phrase, "doctrine is dangerous."

This idea that "doctrine is dangerous" was contagious and quickly spread through the congregation. When challenged to believe something more or believe something differently, members of the congregation would often reply by quoting Paul's words in Colossians 2:8, "See to it that no one takes you captive through hollow and deceptive philosophy, which depends on human tradition and the elemental spiritual forces of this world rather than on Christ." They believed this passage was Biblical proof that doctrine is dangerous and that, instead of thinking about what we ought to believe, we simply need to think about loving Jesus.

There are at least three major problems with this argument.

First, Paul is not speaking against doctrine or philosophy. He is speaking against a certain type of philosophy. Specifically, he is speaking against "deceptive philosophy" that is not dependent on Christ "in whom all the fullness of the Deity lives in bodily form" (Colossians 2:9). In other words, Paul does not believe that "doctrine is dangerous." He believes that *false* doctrine is dangerous. Knowing that false doctrine is dangerous should not move us to think about doctrine less. It should motivate us to think about doctrine all the more in order to ensure that we are not taken captive by the dangers of false doctrine.

The second problem with the argument that "doctrine is dangerous" is that the Bible actually says the exact opposite. Consider the following passages:

> "Watch your life and doctrine closely. Persevere in them, because if you do, you will save both yourself and your hearers" (1 Timothy 4:16).

> "He [an elder] must hold firmly to the trustworthy message as it has been taught, so that he can encourage others by sound doctrine and refute those who oppose it" (Titus 1:9).

> "Do your best to present yourself to God as one approved, a worker who does not need to be ashamed and who correctly handles the word of truth" (2 Timothy 2:15).

In summary, the Bible does not tell us to avoid doctrine but to relentlessly pursue it.

The third problem with the argument "doctrine is dangerous" is that it is impossible to love Jesus well without also loving doctrine. Even worse, we cannot know how greatly and deeply Jesus loves us without doctrine. We cannot know who Jesus is, what Jesus has done, why Jesus did it, what Jesus' work means, or how to know and please Jesus apart from the theological doctrine that reveals and explains these things. We cannot properly respond in faith until we properly interpret God's self-revelation and we cannot properly interpret God's self-revelation unless we are always learning the doctrines of Scripture, evaluating and re-evaluating our beliefs and life in light of them.

This seems to be why Paul's epistles have the format they do. In most of Paul's letters he spends the first half of the letter reminding his readers of deep theological truth about God's love for us and then spends the second half of the letter showing how we ought to love and obey Jesus in light of these theological truths about his love for us. For example, the first 3 chapters of Ephesians are pure doctrine while the last 3 chapters are about how to love and live in light of that doctrine. In Colossians the first 2 chapters focus on doctrine while the last 2 chapters focus on practice. In Romans Paul devotes the first 11 chapters to theological doctrine and spends only the last 5 chapters on how that doctrine should impact our behavior. This is all due to the fact that we cannot love Jesus well through practice until we know Jesus well through doctrine.

The claim that "doctrine is dangerous" is a lie that keeps people from fully knowing Jesus' love for them and fully loving Jesus in response. While it is true that theological doctrine is a terrible end in itself it is a wonderful means to an end, in that it is through theological doctrine that we learn to know Jesus' love for us and be moved to love him well in return. For that reason, we should devote ourselves to regularly studying the Scriptures and the theological works that human authors have given us over the past 2,000 years. Why wouldn't we want to know as much as we can about the one who first loved us so we can love him in response?

DISCUSSION GUIDE: DOCTRINE IS DANGEROUS

CHAPTER SUMMARY
Many are taught to avoid doctrine as if it is harmful. Some even take pride in doing so. Yet the Bible places such heavy emphasis on watching your doctrine and avoiding false ones that it is impossible to love Jesus well without knowing sound doctrine.

DISCUSSION QUESTIONS
1. Often times there is a dichotomy created between love and truth. If you had to error on either side which one would it be? Why?

2. In Scripture there is no conflict between love and truth. How do we see the two working together in the Bible? What guidance does this provide us for our own life?

3. Not all doctrine is true doctrine. How do you differentiate between sound doctrine and false doctrine? What are some examples of common false doctrines? What makes them false?

4. What are some specific examples of doctrines that help you love Jesus better? Explain.

5. Paul warns Timothy to watch his life and doctrine closely because in doing so he will save both himself and his hearers. In what way(s) does watching our life and doctrine save us and our listeners?

YOU DON'T HAVE TO BE PART OF A CHURCH

"You don't have to be part of a church!" Thankfully, this is a lie my own pastor would never think of uttering. He was far more likely to error on the opposite end by telling you that you were at risk of going to Hell if you missed any one of six consecutive nights of revival services. I wish I could say I've never heard any other pastors say, "You don't have to be part of a church!" but I can't. Just recently I attended a memorial service for a man who did not attend church. The pastor of the church shared several stories of times they tried to get the man to attend church but eventually they came to the conclusion that "some people need the church and some people don't" and if someone chooses not to be a part of a church that's okay because, after all, "you don't have to be part of a church as a Christian!" My jaw visibly dropped as I have heard so few pastors publicly proclaim this particular lie before. Yet there can be no debate that while very few pastors have publicly taught this lie, a great number of professing Christians have believed it.

And they shouldn't.

For two reasons: first, because the entire Bible teaches the opposite. Second, because the stakes are dangerously high.

The Commands
God's Word does not teach that "you don't have to be part of a church" but that Christians are to be consistently active members of a local church. It

teaches this both explicitly and implicitly. The clearest explicit teaching is provided in Hebrews 10:24-25, "And let us consider how we may spur one another on toward love and good deeds, not giving up meeting together, as some are in the habit of doing, but encouraging one another—and all the more as you see the Day approaching."

The author of Hebrews, as moved by the Holy Spirit, instructs his Christian audience to gather regularly as the local church. While he does not tell us how often to gather, it is clear that he expects us to be meeting frequently and consistently and that we are to do so with the same group of people, as is seen in his use of "one another." Our relationship with this local body of believers is to be so strong that we will be able to "encourage one another daily" (Hebrews 3:13). The author does not provide these instructions as merely a good idea for some but as a necessity for all. In saying we are to "spur one another on toward love and good deeds...encouraging one another" he is reminding us that we have a responsibility to the other Christians who make up the local church (to encourage them and spur them on toward love and obedience) and that we ourselves need the other Christians who make up the local church (to encourage us and spur us on toward love and obedience). Through these two verses God instructs all Christians to live in this way and not in the way of those who "are in the habit of" not meeting together.

In addition to the explicit instructions of Hebrews 10:24-25 the Scriptures are filled with implicit teachings on this subject. The following is a small selection of such passages, each of which shows that

Christians are expected to be consistently active members of a local church.

> "Have confidence in your leaders and submit to their authority, because they keep watch over you as those who must give an account. Do this so that their work will be a joy, not a burden, for that would be of no benefit to you."
> – Hebrews 13:17

> "There are different kinds of gifts, but the same Spirit distributes them. There are different kinds of service, but the same Lord. There are different kinds of working, but in all of them and in everyone it is the same God at work. Now to each one the manifestation of the Spirit is given for the common good." – 1 Corinthians 12:4-7

> "Make every effort to keep the unity of the Spirit [in the church] through the bond of peace." – Ephesians 4:3

> "Let the message of Christ dwell among you richly as you teach and admonish one another with all wisdom through psalms, hymns and songs from the Spirit, singing to God with gratitude in your hearts." – Colossians 3:16

> "Is anyone among you sick? Let them call the elders of the church to pray over them and anoint them with oil in the name of the Lord." – James 5:14

If a professing Christian is not a part of a local church how can they obey these commands of God? How can you submit to the authority of your church leaders if you are not a part of the church? And how can they keep watch over you if they do not know you? How can you use your spiritual gifts for the common good of the local church if you are not a part of the local church? How can you protect the unity of the Spirit in the local church if you yourself are not in the local church? How can you teach and admonish the rest of the church through song if you do not gather with the church to sing? How can you call for the elders of the church to pray for you in your illness if you are not active in a church that has elders? The answer to every one of these questions is obvious: you can't. And God doesn't intend that you even try.

The Consequences
If a professing Christian is not an active part of a local church they are disobeying the explicit command of Hebrews 10:24-25. Moreover, they are unable to obey the many other commands that require active involvement in a local church in order to be obeyed. This means that they are willfully disobeying dozens of God-given commands simply by not being an active part of a local church.

And this is serious.

Very serious.

First, it is very serious because it casts a significant shadow of doubt over the individual's claim to love Jesus. Jesus himself says, "Whoever has my commands and keeps them is the one who loves me" (John 14:21). That's rather straightforward. Jesus sees a direct link between someone's love for him and someone's obedience to his commands. The person who obeys his commands is the one who loves him. The person who does not, does not. It really is that simple. The Apostle John says the same thing with even harsher language, "We know that we have come to know him if we keep his commands. Those who say, 'I know him,' but do not do what he commands are liars, and the truth is not in them" (1 John 2:3-4). The individual who is physically able to be an active part of a local church, and is not, is willfully disobeying dozens of God-given commands. This calls their profession of faith into serious question. Jesus' counsel to such individuals is simple, "If you love me, keep my commands" (John 14:15).

Second, it is very serious because it hinders the individual's ability to grow as a Christian (if in fact they truly are one). According to the Bible, Christian maturity does not just happen. It happens through the means that God has appointed: the local church.

> "So Christ himself gave the apostles, the prophets, the evangelists, the pastors and teachers, to equip his people for works of service, so that the body of Christ may be built up until we all reach unity in the faith and in the knowledge of the Son of God and become mature, attaining to the whole measure of the fullness of Christ" (Ephesians 4:11-13).

Jesus has given gifted ministers to the local church to help us serve one another "so that the body of Christ (that's the Church) may be built up until we all (as individuals)...become mature." This is why the Apostle Paul chooses to use the metaphor of a body to picture the Church, since each part of the body is dependent on the others. As he writes in 1 Corinthians 12:21,

"The eye cannot say to the hand, 'I don't need you!' And the head cannot say to the feet, 'I don't need you!' As with a physical body, no part of this spiritual body (the Church) can properly grow or properly function without the others.

Third, it is very serious because the local church is God's chosen means of showing off his wisdom and glory to all. Paul writes in Ephesians 3:10, "(God's) intent was that now, through the church, the manifold wisdom of God should be made known." For an individual to fail to play their role in the local church is for that individual to fail to play their role in putting God's wisdom on display. Similarly, it is to fail to play their role in making God known to those who do not know him. In his letter to Titus, Paul gives specific instructions on how certain groups of people are to relate to one another within the context of the local church. He explains that when people in the local church relate to one another properly they "make the teaching about God our Savior attractive" (Titus 2:10) and help ensure "that no one will malign the Word of God" (Titus 2:5).

The Conclusion
Jesus *loves* his Church. He loves his Church so much that he bled and died for her (Ephesians 5:25-27). Why would we not want to love that which is loved so dearly by the Lord we say we so dearly love? Especially when the commands are so clear and the consequences are critical. The claim that as a Christian "you don't have to be part of a church" is a lie. It is, in fact, a vicious lie because it makes some believe they are Christians when in fact they are not, it hinders true Christians from spiritual growth, and it removes people from the context where God most

glorifies himself and makes himself known to the world.

DISCUSSION GUIDE: YOU DON'T HAVE TO BE PART OF A CHURCH

CHAPTER SUMMARY
The local church is not optional for a Christian believer, it is an integral and non-negotiable piece of their personal growth in Jesus and personal obedience to Jesus.

DISCUSSION QUESTIONS
1. There are typically two extreme positions in any argument. In the argument over whether or not a Christian must be in church you have side A, which says you don't have to be part of a church at all, and side B, that says you have to be in church 6 days a week. What are the dangers and misunderstandings in both?

2. Does the type of church you go to matter? If so what should you look for in the local church you attend?

3. One of the biggest roles of the local church is to show off the wisdom and glory of God. How does a church do this? How does your church do this?

4. What are some reasons Christians give for not actively participating in a local church. How do you believe Jesus would answer each of those? (Rely on Scripture as much as possible in your answer).

5. Is it possible for a Christian to grow into maturity apart from the local church? What are some things one misses by not being committed to a local body?

SIN IS SIN

"Sin is sin."

This is a phrase you often hear repeated in church circles. The phrase can be misleading because there is one sense in which it is most certainly true, but there is another sense in which it is absolutely false. It is true if interpreted as meaning all sin offends God, separates us from God, and will be judged by God either on Jesus' cross (for those who believe) or on Jesus' return (for those who do not believe). It is false if what we mean is that all sin is equally offensive to God or has equal consequences. The truth is that God is offended by all sin and God demands consequences for all sin; but precisely how offended he is and precisely what those consequences are depends both on what the sin is and on who commits the sin.

First, the Bible teaches that while all sin is bad, there are some sins that are unquestionably worse than others in God's eyes. This is clear in the Old Testament, especially in God's assessment of various nations and kings. For instance, through his prophet Ezekiel, God rebukes Judah and Israel for their adulterous relationships with Assyria. Yet, in so doing, God assesses Judah's sin as even more wicked than Israel's when he says in Ezekiel 23:11, "Her sister Oholibah [a pejorative term for Judah] saw this, yet in her lust and prostitution she was more depraved than her sister [Israel]." Similar comparative statements are made throughout 1 and 2 Kings. On more than one occasion the sin of one king is said to be greater than those who came before him. The most recognizable example is King Ahab who "did more evil in the eyes of the LORD than any of those before him" (1 Kings 16:30). The author then goes on to list some of his most heinous offenses before concluding that Ahab "did more to arouse the anger of the Lord, the God of Israel, than did all the kings of Israel before him" (1 Kings 16:33). Later, in the story of Manasseh, God compares the evil of both king and nation when he declares first that under Manasseh's leadership the people of Judah "did more evil than the nations the Lord had destroyed before the Israelites" and second that Manasseh himself did "more evil than the Amorites who preceded him" (2 Kings 21:9-11). If it were true that "sin is sin" there would be no standard by which God could call some more evil than others.

The fact that some sins are worse than others in God's eyes is also made clear in the New Testament. Both Jesus and the Apostle John teach there is a particular sin worse than all others. Jesus says, "Truly I tell you, people will be forgiven all their sins and all the blasphemies they utter. But whoever blasphemes against the Holy Spirit will never be forgiven, but is guilty of an eternal sin" (Mark 3:28-29). John may be describing the same core sin when he writes, "If you see any brother or sister commit a sin that does not lead to death, you should pray and God will give them life. I refer to those whose sin does not lead to death. There is a sin that leads to death. I am not saying that you should pray about that" (1 John 5:16). In both cases there is a distinction made between at least two different groups of sin – each of which is an offense to God, but one that is even worse than the others. Further evidence is found in Jesus' pronouncement of judgment on those towns that rejected him.

> "Woe to you, Chorazin! Woe to you, Bethsaida! If the miracles that were performed in you had been performed in Tyre and Sidon, they would have repented long ago in sackcloth and ashes. But I tell you, it will be more bearable for Tyre and Sidon on the day of judgment than for you. And you, Capernaum, will you be lifted up to the skies? No, you will go down to the depths. If the miracles that were performed in you had been performed in Sodom, it would have remained to this day. But I tell you that it will be more bearable for Sodom on the day of judgment than for you" (Matthew 11:21-24).

Jesus' proclamation confirms that "sin is sin" in the sense that all sin will be judged, whether the sin of Chorazin and Bethsaida or Tyre and Sidon. But his speech denies that "sin is sin" in the sense that all sin is equally offensive or faces equal consequences, for "it will be more bearable for Sodom on the day of judgment than for you." This should not surprise us in the least. As human beings we intuitively recognize that that a child abuser should receive worse punishment than someone who goes two miles per-hour over the speed limit. This is because we are created in the image of God, who as the personification of justice hates all sin but does not hate all sin in the same way.

Second, the Bible teaches that while all sin is bad some sins face harsher consequences because of who commits them. Most notably, those who lead God's people face consequences that the rest of God's people do not, both in this present world and at the final judgment.

The unique consequences that church leaders face in this present world include being removed from their office and being publicly corrected, if at any point they fail to meet the leadership qualifications listed in 1 Timothy 3 and Titus 1. These combined lists of leadership qualifications only include two skills – the ability to teach true doctrine and expose false doctrine. Every other qualification is character based. For instance, those who serve as pastors must be faithful to their wife, hospitable, not given to drunkenness, not lovers of money, not quick-tempered. The mere existence of these lists disproves the idea that "sin is sin," for God chooses to list some sins as disqualifying sins and not others. Thus, if a pastor is found sinning in these specific areas they are to be removed from their office and "reproved before everyone" (1 Timothy 5:20). Their sin earns these severe consequences both because of the nature of the sin and because of the nature of their position. As church leaders, their sin causes significant harm to those they lead and brings increased shame upon the gospel in the eyes of a watching world.

Moreover, church leaders face additional consequences in the final judgment, including a harsher judgment. The Apostle James writes, "Not many of you should presume to be teachers, my brothers and sisters, because you know that we who teach will be judged more strictly" (James 3:1). While not explicitly stated, it is likely that they will be judged more strictly because of how their sin impacts those they lead. As Jesus explains in Luke 17:2, "It would be better for you to be thrown into the sea with a millstone tied around your neck than for you to cause one of these little ones to stumble."

In light of all the above, to claim "sin is sin" is to misrepresent God's Word. Worse still, to claim "sin is sin" as a way to minimize the extent of our own wickedness is to deny God his glory. Jesus' finished work on the cross is sufficient for our past, present, and future sin – from the most apparently minor to the most heinous. The more we make our sin appear small or common the more we make Jesus' sacrifice for our sin appear small or common – and it is anything but that. Instead of talking down our sin as if it is no different from anyone else's we ought to talk up our sin, because we are acutely aware of how desperately we need Jesus to save us. That's what the Apostle Paul did. He did not take a "sin is sin" attitude toward his wickedness. He saw it for what it was and, as a result, he saw Jesus' glory magnified.

> "Here is a trustworthy saying that deserves full acceptance: Christ Jesus came into the world to save sinners—of whom I am the worst. But for that very reason I was shown mercy so that in me, the worst of sinners, Christ Jesus might display his immense patience as an example for those who would believe in him and receive eternal life. Now to the King eternal, immortal, invisible, the only God, be honor and glory for ever and ever. Amen" (1 Timothy 1:15-17).

DISCUSSION GUIDE: SIN IS SIN

CHAPTER SUMMARY
While all sins are offensive to God, not all sins are offensive to God in the same way or to the same degree. The Bible clearly shows that some sins are more offensive to God and will be judged more harshly by God.

DISCUSSION QUESTIONS

1. *All* sin will be judged – both the sin of Christians and the sin of those who never become Christians. Describe the two ways in which each is judged.

2. People will often lump sins into the categories of "Big Sins" and "Little Sins." Is this idea supported Biblically? Why or why not? What dangers, if any, arise from segmenting sin like this?

3. What are some sins that are more offensive to God than others? How do we know which sins are the most heinous in the eyes of God?

4. What sins are most offensive in your church culture? Are they the same or different from those that are most offensive to god? If there's a difference, why do you think that is?

5. If we were to believe that all sin is seen and judged equally by God in what ways would that

make our view of the cross, the believer, and the glory of God different from that of Scripture?

GOD WON'T PUT MORE ON YOU THAN YOU CAN BEAR

My pastor had a remedy for suffering in the form of a simple ten-word sentence: "God won't put more on you than you can bear." That was often the extent of his counsel, which, as you might imagine, made his counseling appointments rather brief. If you pay attention to social media, you know how often this counsel is repeated. People are told to hang in there, because—you guessed it—"God won't put more on you than you can bear." That's unfortunate, because it's untrue. God's Word does not teach that he will not put more on you than you can bear.

People often defend this idea by pointing to the Apostle Paul's words in 1 Corinthians 10:13, "No temptation has overtaken you except what is common to us all. And God is faithful; he will not let you be tempted beyond what you can bear. But when you are tempted, he will also provide a way out so that you can endure it." This is a magnificent promise! But it is not a promise that God will not allow us to face unbearable suffering. It is, instead, a promise that God will not allow us to face inescapable temptation. In context, Paul is reminding the Corinthians that God intends for them to learn from Israel's history. The specific lesson he wants them to learn is that they can and must flee idolatry in all its forms.

When people say, "God won't put more on you than you can bear" they are hoping to comfort people who are hurting because of painful life circumstances. Unfortunately, this cliché has a tendency to do the opposite. It can actually cause tremendous discomfort and lead people away from the Gospel, the source of true comfort.

The cliché can cause discomfort by making the suffering person feel that, if they feel overwhelmed, something must be wrong with them. Why are they falling apart under the pressure? Why do the circumstances of their life seem so unbearable? If they believe that "God won't put more on them than they can bear," then they are really left with only two options: to believe they simply don't have enough faith and are failing to trust in God, or to believe that God has abandoned them and left them to face their suffering alone. Either way, they won't be comforted. In fact, their discomfort has only *increased* because now they fear not only whatever circumstance they are facing, but also that they have lost necessary faith in God or that God has abandoned them.

The truth is, God often puts more on his children than they can bear. The Apostle Paul himself, who wrote 1 Corinthians 10:1, discusses his own unbearable experiences in his second letter to the Corinthians. After describing some of the sufferings he and his team faced on their gospel mission he explains, "We do not want you to be uninformed, brothers and sisters, about the troubles we experienced in the province of Asia. We were under great pressure, *far beyond our ability to endure*, so that we despaired of life itself" (2 Corinthians 1:8, emphasis mine). Paul would not dare say, "God won't put more on you than you can bear." He knew first hand what it's like to suffer beyond what you can humanly endure. His suffering was so intense that he "despaired of life itself."

And Paul is not the only biblical example. Elijah faced challenging circumstances that led him to conclude, "I have had enough, Lord" and then ask for God to take his life (1 Kings 19:4). The Angel of the Lord did not deny Elijah's claim. Rather, the Angel of the Lord acknowledged the truth of his words and declared that Elijah's circumstances were "too much" for him (1 Kings 19:7). Moses likewise faced suffering that was beyond his ability to bear and voiced his frustrations to God in prayer. "I cannot carry all these people by myself; *the burden is too heavy for me.* If this is how you are going to treat me, please go ahead and kill me" (Numbers 11:14-15a, emphasis mine). As with Elijah, the Lord did not disagree with Moses' assessment. He responded by relieving some of Moses' burden. In addition, the Psalms are filled with the cries of desperate men, overwhelmed by the sufferings of life. Even a quick glance at psalms like Psalm 6, 42, and 88 reveal God's people suffering beyond what they can bear.

Telling suffering people, "God won't put more on you than you can bear!" tends to lead them away from the means to true comfort God has provided. The truth is, God at times intentionally gives you more than you can bear by yourself so you will rely on God and God's people. This is the argument Paul makes when he shares his unbearable experience with the Corinthians. After explaining the suffering was more than he could bear he writes, "But this happened that we might not rely on ourselves but on God" (2 Corinthians 1:9). He is explaining that God intentionally gave them more than they could bear so that they would depend on his strength instead of their own.

Later in the same letter Paul shares a similar experience. After repeatedly asking the Lord to heal his unbearable physical pain, Paul writes that the Lord replied, "My grace is sufficient for you, for my power is made perfect in weakness." Those words brought Paul great comfort. So much so that he decided, "Therefore I will boast all the more gladly about my weaknesses, so that Christ's power may rest on me" (2 Corinthians 12:9).

For Paul and for others it is a comfort to know that God bears the burdens that we cannot. We will never experience this comfort if we live as if "God won't put more on you than you can bear." In reality, God often gives us more than we can bear and invites us to bring the excess weight to him and to his people. This is why the Apostle Peter urges us to "cast all your anxiety on him because he cares for you" (1 Peter 5:7) and Paul encourages the church community to "carry one another's burdens" (Galatians 6:2).

The entire message of the Bible is that you cannot bear your own burdens and that Jesus loved you enough to come to earth and bear them for you. Jesus says it bluntly: "apart from me you can do nothing" (John 15:5), but then offers the words of ultimate comfort: "Come to me, all who labor and are heavy laden, and I will give you rest. Take my yoke upon you, and learn from me, for I am gentle and lowly in heart, and you will find rest for your souls" (Matthew 11:28-29). In light of that we ought never say, "God won't put more on you than you can bear." Instead, we ought always say, "God won't put more on you than *he* can bear."

DISCUSSION GUIDE: GOD WON'T PUT MORE ON YOU THAN YOU CAN BEAR

CHAPTER SUMMARY
God does not promise to never give you more than you can bear. The whole storyline of the Bible actually says the exact opposite. Yet God does promise that precisely because you will face more than you can bear he will carry your burdens for you.

DISCUSSION QUESTIONS

1. In his faithfulness, God always provides us with an opportunity to escape from sin when tempted. Describe a time when this was true for you.

2. Why do you think we are so attracted to the idea that "God will not give you more than you can bear"? What does that reveal about our faith?

3. Can you think of a time in your life where you were given more than you could bear? If so, what positive things, if any, came out of that painful experience?

4. When God lays more on us than we can bear we are urged to press into him and into the local church. Has there been a time when your local church has helped you to carry a burden?

How did this experience affect you as a believer?

5. Christ carried the ultimate burden of our sins on the cross. A burden we could never carry. As a group, take some time to reflect upon this truth and worship him because of it.

FREQUENTLY ASKED QUESTIONS

Why Such a Controversial Title?
The title we chose for the book was intentionally provocative. We wanted a title that would motivate the people we most wanted to read the book to take a look. We could not accomplish that with a title like, Some False Teachings You Believe, as the people we most wanted to help would not be aware they might need such a book. Yet, understandably, some have misinterpreted the book as being anti-pastor because of the title. I'm grateful this second edition gives me the opportunity to clarify.

The book is not anti-pastor.

I am not anti-pastor.

I myself am a pastor and have been since 2006. The Bible tells us that pastors are a God-given gift to the Church. Their purpose is to equip us to serve one another so we all together grow to full maturity in Jesus Christ (Ephesians 4:11-13). We are to honor them (1 Timothy 5:17) and submit to them (Hebrews 13:17). Yet we are never to do this at the expense of honoring and submitting to Jesus Christ. When a pastor is leading us away from Jesus Christ, we are to honor and submit to Jesus as the Pastor of Pastors (1 Peter 5:4). The provocative book title is a reflection of my desire to do that and help others do that.

Who Do You Think You Are?
A Christian.

I don't say that trying to be clever, I say that with sincerity. I am a Christian and, like all other Christians, I am called to evaluate the teachings of our leaders through the lens of the Word of God. The Bible does not just encourage this, it praises this. The Holy Spirit inspired Luke to write this in Acts 17:11, "Now the Berean Jews were of more noble character than those in Thessalonica, for they received the message with great eagerness and examined the Scriptures every day to see if what Paul said was true."

This verse teaches us three things about how we ought to respond to the teaching of Christian leaders.

1. We ought to respond with eagerness to receive the message. We should never sit under Christian teaching with a closed or critical heart before we have even heard the message. We should give our brothers and sisters the benefit of the doubt, and be eager to hear God speak through them.

2. We ought to examine what we hear in light of the Scriptures. As Christian teachers present their understanding of the Word, we should be sure to evaluate their teaching in light of the teachings of Scripture. Where their message is consistent with Scripture we must submit, where it contradicts Scripture we must reject it.

3. We must do the above in the context of Christian community. We are not the judges of what Scripture does or does not teach. The Christian Church throughout all time and places is. The Bereans evaluated Paul's teaching in Christian community, and we must do the same.

If we do all three of the things above the Bible says we possess "noble character." If we do not open ourselves up to receive the Word with eagerness, we are hard-hearted. If we receive the word with eagerness without confirming its veracity in Scripture, we are foolish. If we set ourselves up as the individual judges of what is or is not biblical, we are arrogant. Yet if we imitate the Bereans we, like them, are of noble character.

The book is the product of my attempts to do this and a tool I hope helps many others do the same.

What Church Background Are You From and/or Talking About in the Book?

As mentioned in the original introduction, this book is not about any particular pastor. It is based on a composite of pastors I have encountered in my time as a Christian. These pastors come from a wide variety of churches throughout the United States and elsewhere. Nevertheless, many have read the book and assumed I am aiming my critique at a certain type of church.

I am not.

The lies in this book are not limited to a particular denomination, a particular culture, or any other particular sub-group of Christians. If you have not been exposed to them personally, you are very fortunate. Yet this does not mean they cannot be found in churches that appear very similar to yours. If you have been exposed to them personally, you are not alone. You can find one or more of these clichés in all sorts of places influencing all sorts of people.

The problem is not with any particular type of church. The problem is with false teaching, anywhere and everywhere it exists. The solution is the truth of the Gospel, and there is not a single denomination or culture that can claim exclusive ownership of that.

What if My Pastor Teaches These Lies?
This is the most common and most important question I've been asked. If you read the book and are convinced that your pastor is mishandling the Scriptures, what are you supposed to do?

This question is very difficult to answer in writing, as each circumstance is different. There is no blanket answer that can adequately and accurately address every situation. For this reason, you very much need to lean on the revelation of Scripture, the guidance of the Holy Spirit, and the wise counsel of gospel-saturated Christians. I firmly believe that God can and will guide you through these resources if you are willing to seek them and hear them. That said, there are some general principles I can provide to add to the far-more-valuable resources you already have.

First, recognize that the clichés in this book are not equally destructive. For example, I believe "This is God's House," "I Have Peace About this Decision," and "God Won't Put More On You Than You Can Bear" are false, and those who believe them miss out on some of the comfort and joy the gospel offers. Yet I do not believe these teachings are central enough or destructive enough to justify leaving a church. If these were the worst teachings my pastor offered, I would gladly submit to him and faithfully give myself to his church.

On the other hand, there are several clichés that are far more damaging. For instance, "Speak it Into Existence" puts man in the place of God and God in the place of man. "God Wants You to Be Rich" and "God Heals All Who Have Faith" similarly encourage idolatry by moving our focus from Jesus and the true riches he provides to the god of worldly prosperity. If my pastor were to teach these things, I would not be able to continue submitting to him as a member of his church.

Second, it may be helpful to ask, "Can I continue to invite people to this church with confidence they will hear the gospel of Jesus and learn how to follow him?" If the answer is "yes," then it likely does not make sense to leave your church without a specific call from God or the discovery of unrepentant sin in the leadership. If the answer is "no," your current church may not be a good place for you long-term, as you are commanded to evangelize and make disciples within the context of your local church.

Third, I encourage you to ask yourself, "Can I continue to submit to my pastor as the appointed leader of the church?" God commands you to submit to your leaders. This means you are expected to submit to your pastor and his leadership even if you take issue with some of his teaching. If the teachings you disagree with are not central to the faith or significantly damaging to Christians, you may find that you are able to submit to him in good conscience. In fact, you should expect that no matter what church you attend you will need to submit to a pastor with whom you disagree on some points. Yet if your pastor's teachings are central to the faith or significantly damaging to Christians, you may be unable to submit to him in good conscience. In this case, it is best for both you and your pastor that you find a church where you can.

Lastly, remember that every pastor has his blind spots. You will never find one who comes remotely close to perfection. Because of this, you should prioritize the gospel. The best church for you is a church where the gospel message of who Jesus is and what Jesus has done is proclaimed weekly through the preaching, singing, counseling - everything - and where church leadership is aiming to bring their imperfect lives in accord with the message they preach.

ABOUT THE AUTHOR

Cole Brown (MABTS, MAT) has been planting and pastoring churches since 2006 following his first career in the music industry. He, his wife, and their two children currently live between Portland, Oregon and Mexico City, Mexico, where they are missionaries who work to help start and strengthen churches throughout Latin America.

He is the author of several books and also blogs for organizations such as Humble Beast, The Gospel Coalition, Witness and others.

His Spanish-language resources are available at colebrown.es.

CONCENTRATED TRUTH

Good theology is essential to good living.

Therefore, it should not be relegated to the realm of abstract theory and hard-to-read books. Good theology should be practical for daily life and accessible to everyone. This is why Cole Brown and Humble Beast together created *Concentrated Truth.*

The books in the *Concentrated Truth* series bring heavy theological concepts into our daily language and daily lives. They do so in small and easy-to-read packages aimed at transforming the way you think and live. Each book also includes a free discussion guide so you can experience such transformation in the context in which God transforms us: the Christian community.

TITLES INCLUDE:

Daddy Issues: How God Heals Wounds Caused by Absent, Abusive & Aloof Fathers

The Gospel Is...: Defining the Most Important Message in the World

Lies My Pastor Told Me: Confronting Church Clichés with the Gospel

Lies Hip Hop Told Me: Confronting Hip Hop Slogans with the Gospel

Made in the USA
Coppell, TX
17 July 2023